BRIGHT NOTES

THE VICTORIAN POETS

Intelligent Education

Nashville, Tennessee

BRIGHT NOTES: The Victorian Poets
www.BrightNotes.com

No part of this publication may be used or reproduced in any manner whatsoever without written permission, except in the case of brief quotations in critical articles and reviews. For permissions, contact Influence Publishers http://www.influencepublishers.com.

ISBN: 978-1-645424-78-9 (Paperback)
ISBN: 978-1-645424-79-6 (eBook)

Published in accordance with the U.S. Copyright Office Orphan Works and Mass Digitization report of the register of copyrights, June 2015.

Originally published by Monarch Press.
Peter F. Mullany; Margaret K. Mullany, 1963
2020 Edition published by Influence Publishers.

Interior design by Lapiz Digital Services. Cover Design by Thinkpen Designs.

Printed in the United States of America.

Library of Congress Cataloging-in-Publication Data forthcoming.
Names: Intelligent Education
Title: BRIGHT NOTES: The Victorian Poets
Subject: STU004000 STUDY AIDS / Book Notes

CONTENTS

1)	The Victorian Poets	1
2)	The Victorian Poets: Textual Analysis	12
	Alfred, Lord Tennyson	12
	Robert Browning	38
	Matthew Arnold	72
	Dante Gabriel Rossetti	95
	William Morris	106
	Algernon Charles Swinburne	113
	Gerard Manley Hopkins	123
	The Minor Victorian Poets	133
3)	Essay Questions and Answers	149
4)	Bibliography & Guide to Further Research	162

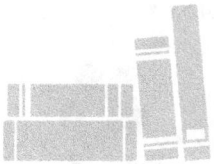

THE VICTORIAN POETS

INTRODUCTION

THE VICTORIAN PERIOD

This period spans the reign of Queen Victoria (1837-1901). The term Victorian is used in its widest sense to designate the body of literature written during these years and to suggest the particular qualities and attitudes of that literature. Modern usage of the term suggests a sense of prudery, false modesty, or empty respectability which it is felt characterized the nineteenth century. This latter pejorative use of Victorian is really based on an exaggerated response to the high standards of "decency" and the moral earnestness of the period. It is true that Victorian writers were often very cautious with regard to profanity and matters of sex, but to reject them on this score would be totally unfair. Indeed, Victorian literature reflects the tremendous social, political, and religious upheavals of the age, and we today are the heirs to many of their findings. If anything, the Victorian period is one of great change, an age of transition, and the literature of the period reveals to us the great tensions and pressures that existed beneath the surface optimism and serenity, so often referred to as Victorian.

IMPORTANT DATES

Some of the important dates and events of the period can be listed to help in describing the age:

(1) 1832 - The First Reform Bill
(2) 1837 - Victoria becomes Queen of England
(3) 1846 - The Corn Laws repealed
(4) 1851 - Prince Albert presents the Great Exhibition in London. The erection of the Crystal Palace testifies to the industrial achievement of England.
(5) 1854-1856 - War against Russia in the Crimea
(6) 1859 - Charles Darwin's *Origin of Species* published
(7) 1870-71 - Franco-Prussian War
(8) 1901 - Queen Victoria's death

SOCIAL AND POLITICAL CHANGE

England had been ruled by an aristocratic, Anglican group down through the eighteenth century. The Neo-Classical period of the late seventeenth and eighteenth centuries emphasized elegance, grace, urbanity and wit-all indicative of a literature appealing largely to the aristocracy. However, a Puritan middle class had been emerging since the early seventeenth century and in the Victorian period this class emerges as a powerful political and social force. Romanticism, in part responding to the appeal of the French Revolution (1789), had stressed individualism and had expressed sympathy for the isolated masses striving for political and economic freedom. Victorianism developed this Romantic interest in a social sense, stressing the need for an ordered society wherein the individual might find his rightful place. Unlike Romanticism which so often stressed the value of individual experience in itself, the Victorian writers were concerned with the public character and the public importance of literature. Thus, for example, Alfred, Lord Tennyson's poetry provided the age with moral reflections on heroes and thereby offered instruction to his readers.

THE REFORM BILL OF 1832

This bill extended the right to vote to members of the rising industrial middle class. The invention of the steam engine, the spinning jenny, and the power loom in the late eighteenth century contributed to the growth of England as an industrial power.

Victorian liberalism championed the rights of the upper capitalist group of the middle class - the new captains of industry - against the old landed aristocracy. The Reform Bill marked a tremendous shift in political power and gave rise to at least a partially democratic form of government. Thus one of the great changes that sets the Victorian age apart from others was the arrival of big business and the spread of middle class government.

VICTORIAN LIBERALISM

The social philosophy of Victorian liberalism championed the rights of the middle class and greatly helped to secure the reforms instituted in 1832. Today we speak of "liberals as those who believe in the right and duty of government to establish and secure the welfare and happiness of all citizens. However, the liberal philosophy of the nineteenth century was in many ways opposite to our understanding of the term.

The rise of middle class government and of big business are - as indicated above - characteristics which set the nineteenth century apart. Liberalism of the period was indebted to the political and social philosophies found in the eighteenth century writings of the philosophers John Locke in England and Jean Rousseau in France. The Declaration of Independence also influenced Victorian liberalism. In the political sphere, liberalism sought the liberties of all citizens and advocated that government should restrict its functions to the maintenance of public order. In short its attitude as regards government was one of laissez faire, or "hand off"!

UTILITARIANISM

Connected with Victorian liberalism was the philosophy of Utilitarianism. Its chief exponent was Jeremy Bentham (1772-1832). Utilitarianism expressed the belief that men are motivated by self-interest and that they should seek as much pleasure in life as possible. The utilitarians desired to test all institutions - government, church, and law - to see if they were useful, that is, to see if they contributed to the greatest happiness of the greatest number of men. The Benthamites succeeded in reforming the Civil Service in England, and they further rejected religion as an outdated superstition. Religion, as we shall see, was another great problem in the Victorian period.

VICTORIAN SOCIETY

Industrial revolution and the rise of middle class democracy characterize the society of nineteenth century England. Utilitarianism and liberalism proposed a view of man as an economic creature motivated by self-interest. Thomas Carlyle (1795-1881), the essayist and historian, coined the phrase "cash-nexus" (cash link or bond) which summed up the relationship of man to fellow man. A society now ruled largely by wealthy industrialists offered the desire for money as one of the greatest goals in life. Along with a desire for money went a desire for social advancement - Charles Dickens' (1812-1870) *Great Expectations* (1860) is a novel whose title and story tell of this desire. It became a "duty" to become a gentleman. A mood of optimism permeated Victorian England. England was the first nation of the world to become industrialized. During the century the population rose from two million inhabitants when Victoria became Queen to six and one-half million at her death. England remained unchallenged as the leading world power until late in the century when Germany and the United States both emerged to challenge her leadership. Temperance, industry, frugality, self-reliance became the virtues of this middle class society. The pace of growth was rapid and faith was placed in material progress. Perhaps Thomas Babington Macaulay (1800-1859), essayist and historian, best expressed the mood of optimism when he referred to the English people as "the greatest and most highly civilized people that ever the world saw." Macaulay prophesied of the future in his "Southey's Colloquies" (1829):

> **If we were to prophesy that in the year 1930 a population of fifty millions, better fed, clad, and lodged than the English of our time, will cover these islands. that machines constructed on principles yet undiscovered will be in every house, that there will be no highways but railroads, no travelling but by steam, that our debt, vast as it seems to us, will appear to our great-grandchildren a trifling encumberance, which might easily be paid off in a year or two, many people would think us insane.**

Macaulay's optimism is echoed by Tennyson in his poem "Locksley Hall"; however, Tennyson did not always write so enthusiastically of industrial progress.

THE REACTION

No age can be characterized safely by neat and pithy generalizations. History is complex and the Victorian period is no exception. While some advocated belief in material progress, there were others who were thoroughly dismayed with the events of the period. Macaulay praised industrial progress, but Tennyson struck a different note in "Locksley Hall" when he wrote: "Slowly comes a hungry people, as a lion, creeping nigher, / Glares at one that nods and winks behind a slowly dying fire." Progress also brought horrible abuses. While the captains of industry grew rich, thousands of laborers starved and suffered awful brutalities. Abject poverty existed alongside great wealth. Records of the period indicate that children of from six to eight years of age worked ten to twelve hours a day. Women worked until the very last stages of pregnancy. Housing for the lower-middle class and for the poor was terrible, and many were forced to live in cellars or to crowd into small rooms. Elizabeth Barrett Browning (1806-1861) was a passionate humanitarian who worked to improve child labor conditions and her political and humanitarian poems reflect this interest. Charles Dickens' novel *Oliver Twist* (1838), gave a realistic portrait of workhouse conditions.

TORY PATERNALISM AND SOCIALISM

Political response to the social situation took two forms: Tory Paternalism and Socialism. The laissez faire philosophy encouraged the government to stand by and allow the dreadful conditions mentioned above. Tory Paternalism emphasized that the government had a responsibility to act for the welfare of the people. This was an aristocratic response to problems and also a reaction against liberalism. Government measures such as the repeal of the Corn Laws in 1846 helped to ease the situation. This measure greatly reduced the tariffs and allowed for free trade and the importation of food. Socialism, though not the dominant voice of the period nor the most effective, was still a strong opposition force. It sought government control of utilities, land, and industry. The Fabian Society became the important Socialist group. The extreme form of Socialism was Communism. The *Communist Manifesto* of Karl Marx and Friedrich Engels appeared in 1847, and Marx's *Capital* appeared in 1867, 1885, 1895. A second reform bill was ultimately passed in 1867, and the right to vote was extended to the working classes. Labor thus became a powerful political force.

RELIGION

The emergence of religious doubt is another characteristic of the Victorian period. The Benthamites rejected religion as superstition and were met by the conservative voice of the Oxford Movement, led by John Henry Cardinal Newman (1801-1890), one of the great prose writers of the period and author of *Apologia Pro Vita Sua* (Apology in behalf of his life) and *The Idea of a University*. Newman, who later became a Roman Catholic, defended the High Church and dogmatic, institutional religion against its enemies. Thomas Carlyle remarked that his was an age "at once destitute of faith and terrified at scepticism." Carlyle offered a doctrine of work to his age as a substitute religion and closed his essay "Everlasting Yea" with the command "Produce, Produce!"

Traditional religion and belief in a supernatural reality were often supplanted by a religion of humanity. The service of man replaced the service of God. Another substitute religion was that based on the Ideal of Hero Worship - thus the preoccupation in Victorian literature with legendary heroes. In a sense hero-worship was a reaction against the anti-intellectual, materialistic spirit of the age, and it was hoped that the hero would offer spiritual nourishment and an ideal of life.

SCIENCE

Advances in geology and astronomy indicated to man the age and expanse of his universe. Charles Darwin's *The Origin of Species* (1859) was a landmark in biology and proclaimed the theory of evolution, or natural selection. The conflict with the Biblical account of man's origin became a celebrated controversial issue. In the 1860's evolution and Biblical Criticism based on the new discoveries of science and using scientific method questioned traditional orthodoxies. The foundations of religious belief were shaken, and Matthew Arnold remarked there was "not a creed which is not shaken, not an accredited dogma which is not shown to be questionable, not a received tradition which does not threaten to dissolve."

LITERATURE

The literature of the Victorian period defies neat and tidy generalizations. Nineteenth century England was marked by considerable diversity, and Victorian literature reflects this diversity. However, it is possible to assess within certain limits and with some caution the "temper" of the literature. Victorian literature is often remarked for its solemnity, and many

Victorian writers did believe that they were "prophets" offering moral and practical instruction. Matthew Arnold thought of poetry as a new religion and stated that the function of poetry was to interpret life for us, to console us, to sustain us." Part of this seriousness was a reaction against the verbal beauties of the Romantic poets Percy Bysshe Shelley (1792-1822) and John Keats (1795-1821), and against the volutionary spirit and the wild and passionate heroes of George Gordon, Lord Byron (1788-1824).

The term "Evangelical" is often applied to Victorian literature and it is a term that goes back to the eighteenth century Low Church teachings of John Wesley, the English clergyman and founder of Methodism. As applied to literature "evangelical" characterizes the rigorous code of puritan morality and the enthusiastic interest in reform so predominant in Victorian life. This puritan code was largely a middle class product emphasizing the practical virtues of hard work and worldly success. It required abstention from worldly pleasures and ultimately produced a kind of conformity. Thus one should note Victorian earnestness or seriousness, its emphasis upon puritan morality, and finally its concern for commercial and worldly success. Respectability - agreement with an external code of social behavior - became a leading value of the period.

THE VICTORIAN DILEMMA

The puritan code greatly influenced Victorian literature and accounted for the writer's painstaking efforts to avoid material that would bring a blush to young ladies' cheeks. Perhaps more important was the desire for instruction rather than entertainment. This posed a dilemma for the writer. He was tossed between an obligation to his art and the demands made upon him by his readers. Thus the diversity of Victorian literature is in part attributable to this dilemma and to the individual writer's response to it.

In an age tossed between belief and doubt, the writer sought to instruct and to inspire his readers or he offered them escape by portraying remote times in Greece, medieval England, or in the land of lotus-eating as in Tennyson's "The Lotus Eaters" (1842). Often one can see the tensions between these two appeals co-existing in the same work. Thus Matthew Arnold's *Sohrab and Rustum*, Tennyson's *Idylls of the King*, and Morris's *Earthly Paradise* present both escape and heroic adventure and also an appeal for heroic action.

PRE-RAPHAELITISM

This movement was a romantic reaction against the ugly, noisy world of industrial England. It was established in 1848 and was headed by Dante Gabriel Rossetti (1828-1882). The group was composed of writers and painters who sought to return to the simple devotion to nature which they found in Italian religious art before Raphael (1483-1520), an Italian painter and architect. In their work these poets and painters tried to adhere to the minutest detail of nature and thereby rejected all **conventions** which were designed to heighten effects artificially. They sought freedom from rules. The poetry of the group is characterized by pictorial elements, the use of symbolism, sensuousness, experiments in meter and rhythm, and attention to minute detail. Pre-Raphaelite interest in the medieval and the supernatural as subjects indicates their desire to escape to a more beautiful past. Rossetti's poem "Blue Damozel" (1850), and Morris' "Blue Closet" are poems which reflect the pictorial side of this movement. Algernon Charles Swinburne's "Garden of Proserpine" reflects the musical side.

The work of the Pre-Raphaelites indicates the literary variety of the Victorian Period. The student of Victorian literature must be cautioned against any attempt to judge an individual author according to a preconceived plan. Each writer must be examined individually to discover his unique merits and his unique insights into the meaning of experience. The Victorian poets, like the poets of every age, sought to discover the significance of their times and their poetry offers us a variety of insights into a paradoxical time of optimism, serenity, doubt, fear, and skepticism -

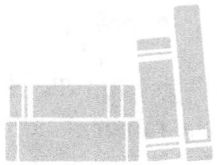

THE VICTORIAN POETS

TEXTUAL ANALYSIS

ALFRED, LORD TENNYSON

....

INTRODUCTION

More so than any of his major contemporaries Tennyson has suffered a marked decline in critical and popular appeal. Ironically, some of the very qualities which endeared him to his Victorian public for more than half a century have been responsible for the decline in the appreciation and estimate of his poetry since his death. In the twentieth century Tennyson has long suffered from the stigma of being summed up and described as "Victorian," with all the **connotations** that term still has for the modern reader. To his detractors, and they seemed to be in the majority until the last decade or two, Tennyson epitomizes the very sensibility of his age, particularly its defects.

SPOKESMAN OF ERA

There are several reasons for the identification of Tennyson with the Victorian age. His life (1809-1892) all but spans the century, and his poetical career runs almost parallel to the most influential years of Queen Victoria's reign (1837-1901). Tennyson was very productive, and the volume of his work is much greater than that of Matthew Arnold, the poet closest to Tennyson as an interpreter of his time.

CURRENT REPUTATION

The reaction to all things Victorian, which was at its height in the early decades of the twentieth century, is now undergoing a revision. The thinking reader can no longer dismiss the era as one of complacency, prudery, and shallow optimism concealing a cowardly fear to face the truth about reality. Tennyson has benefited from this re-evaluation of his era. He has also profited from the approaches in contemporary criticism which emphasize the literary values of the poem and go far beyond looking at it as primarily a philosophical or biographical statement adorned with pretty but extraneous description. Using more aesthetic criteria for evaluating poetry modern critics generally agree that Tennyson, in a fair proportion of his work, is a master craftsman. He is important not only for his proficiency in creating beautiful **imagery** and rhythms, which in themselves are not sufficient to determine the success of a poem. He has also contributed a body of poems to the language which excel in the integral combination of their elements into a whole that evokes moods of latent dramatic tension and ambivalence conveyed through the subtle use of paradox and symbol.

In regard to Tennyson's reputation one thing is fairly clear, and not uncommon in the history of literature. It is likely to be founded for posterity on many poems which were not particularly important or popular in their day. Conversely many of the pieces most well known in his lifetime are today hardly remembered and not likely to be revived in the future.

EARLY LIFE

Tennyson was born in 1809 in Somesby in Lincolnshire in the north of England. Although quite precocious and showing an early talent for poetry, his childhood was unhappy. His father, the Reverend George Tennyson, the rector of a small parish church, was a cultivated and scholarly man but subject to deep fits of depression and violence. The Tennyson children (nine out of twelve lived to maturity) were all bright and possessed to some degree the literary talent of their brother. But they also shared the despondent nature of their father, and Alfred was no exception. Fortunately he was better able to control his melancholy and make it productive, but it remained a characteristic of his personality and poetry throughout his life. It can be noted in the sense of brooding pessimism which marks his short lyrics and challenges the overt confidence of some of his longer works. Tennyson is able to overcome his melancholy at times and express hope, however tremulous. But he never laughs. Considering his vast output Tennyson's canon is rather remarkable for its lack of humor or genuine joy. He does not have in any degree the sense of **irony** and comic detachment which marks the poetry of Pope. He does not even share the stark objectivity of Byron, who could take the world and himself as seriously as Tennyson but who could also step back and say of himself and other men, "Lord, what fools these mortals be!"

AMBIVALENCE IN TENNYSON'S POETRY

The tension in Tennyson's poems between a rationalistic statement of well-being and reconciliation and an underlying emotional tone of despair, conveyed through **imagery** and rhythm, produces the peculiar ambivalence which is so marked a quality of Tennyson's poetry. It appears in many variations. The conflicts between faith and science, desire and conscience, the past and the future, progress and deterioration, art and morality are just a few of the **themes** found in his poetry which testify to an early and lifelong interior conflict.

THE VICTORIAN COMPROMISE

This sense of the individual caught between emotionally irreconcilable forces, which he is not capable of either synthesizing or identifying with one side or the other, is part of the "Victorian Dilemma." Modern readers are often impatient not so much with the despair expressed by the poet, but with the frequent compromise arrived at as a solution to the anguish of being in doubt. Rather than suffer the despair which would result from acknowledging that the Christian faith is untenable, they arrive at a belief based solely on desire. These readers feel that Tennyson, like his age, in such poems as "Locksley Hall", "In Memoriam" and "Maud", for example, raises the problem but never really honestly explores what it means to an individual to find that he must not only live in a hostile world but must also live at war with himself. Once recognizing that there is a tension between an individual's desires and his duties, between his instincts and his conscience, between his faith and his reason, between his art and his social responsibilities, Tennyson, like his fellow Victorians, it is charged, gives lip service to a belief in self-restraint and dedication to the social order because he is afraid to face the ugly truths that might be found if the questions were further pursued. Tennyson, it is true, is sometimes pat and complacent in his answers to profound questions, but many passages in the three poems just mentioned reveal genuine struggle and cannot be called superficial.

EDUCATION

Tennyson used his father's large library to great advantage and knew both the classics and the great English poets at an early age. Like his brothers, he wrote poetry at an early age, and it is notable that his juvenile poems announce the **themes** of deprivation, loneliness, and despair which are so characteristic of his mature work. A few of the titles in the 1827 volume of verse *Poems by Two Brothers* (written in collaboration with his brother Charles and published anonymously) indicate this early melancholy: "The Exile's Return," "The Outcast," "Remorse."

In 1827 Tennyson went up to Trinity College, Cambridge, where he seems to have profited more from the friendship of a distinguished group of young intellectuals called The Apostles than from the formal academic fare of the University. Among the most important of these friends was Arthur Hallam. Hallam and the other young men were interested in the most avant garde thinking of the day. They introduced Tennyson to the work of two almost unknown poets at the time, Shelley and Keats, as well as to the transcendental idealism of Coleridge.

Although studying in an atmosphere permeated by Romantic ideas Tennyson and his friends were already conscious of the conflict inherent in the philosophy of the Romantic poets. Tennyson could not make the total commitment to an individual vision of beauty which characterized Keats or Shelley. He, like the Victorian Age itself, was becoming aware of the demands of the social order which could not be forever subservient to the will of the individual. Throughout his life Tennyson could not quite make up his mind as to whether his duty as a poet was to follow his own private vision of reality or to assume the role of moralist and teacher for the enlightenment of the public.

FIRST VOLUME OF POETRY, 1830, 1832

Gaining confidence and widening his horizons under the inspiration of The Apostles, the massively built but painfully shy poet was bold enough to publish his first independent book of poems in 1830, *Poems, Chiefly Lyrical*. In 1832 there followed a second volume, *Poems*. Both these early works express the diverse aspects of the poet's sensibility. The most marked tendency, expressed in the lyrics such as "Mariana," "The Lady of Shalott," "Oenone," and "The Lotus Eaters," is toward a poetry that achieves its effect by mood and atmosphere. The influence of Keats in terms of lush **imagery** and that of Shelley in regard to variety of musical rhythms is evident.

MYTHS AND LEGENDS

In the above mentioned poems Tennyson uses the classical myths and the legends associated with King Arthur and his Court as subject matter, and structural devices through which he conveys the more modern **themes** of estrangement, resignation and vague despair. He continued this use of mythical material throughout his career, and his exploration and experimentation with such material antedates its use by such great modern poets as Yeats and Eliot.

SYMBOLISM

In the lyrics in these first two volumes Tennyson also reveals in his treatment of **imagery** and rhythm a technique which moves toward modern symbolism. In "Mariana," for example, which is a **ballad** , he is not interested in developing character or telling a story, as **ballads** usually do, but in creating an atmosphere of intense loneliness. All the individual details combine with the weary music of the **refrain** to create a single image, a symbol, which communicates the sense of marked isolation. "The Sea-Fairies" and "The Lotus-Eaters" also utilize this technique and convey a longing for a dreamlike state of resignation and abandonment of the world and its demands. Tennyson's emphasis on the **themes** of isolation, loss and despair, untouched by any optimism, also anticipates the major **themes** of modern literature.

POEMS DEALING WITH THE FUNCTION OF ART

The second group of poems in these two volumes deals with the function of art, and they tend to be rather **didactic** statements on the poets's moral and social commitments, as found in "The Poet," "The Palace of Art," "You Ask Me, Why." These poems tend toward more explicit statement to make their point than the lyrics, which, although they use the framework of legend, are more subjective and evocative. Probably showing the influence of Shelley, Tennyson in these **didactic** poems envisions the artist as the discoverer of truth and the agent of human freedom. "The Palace of Art," his most important early statement on the relation of art to daily life, attempts to express the dangers of a life dedicated to the pursuit of Beauty. It is not a very good poem, as its message is confused and too loosely related to the abundant description to make it an integrated whole. It is almost as if the poem in its dichotomy between lush **imagery** and **didactic** statement unconsciously mirrors the unsolved conflict in the poet's mind. Unlike Keats, Tennyson could never say without qualification, "Beauty is truth, Truth Beauty - That's all/Ye know on Earth and all ye need to know."

DEATH OF HALLAM, 1833

Tennyson's first two volumes of poetry were not well received by the critics. He was attacked as "obscure" and "affected." But a much greater sorrow was soon to afflict the poet than the censure of the critics. Having enjoyed the closest friendship with Hallam even after the poet had left Cambridge in 1831 because of financial difficulty, Tennyson was deeply affected by his death in 1833. He began writing his great tribute to Hallam, the **elegy** "In Memoriam," soon after his death, but it was not completed for publication until 1850.

DECADE OF SILENCE, 1832-1842

Hallam's death ushered in a period of silence in which Tennyson published no poetry until 1842. He suffered from severe financial distress during this time which prevented his marriage to Emily Sellwood, with whom he had fallen in love in 1836 but could not marry until 1850. Although despondent to the point where his friends felt he would never write again, actually Tennyson seems to have spent the decade revising his early poems and trying to perfect his art in solitude.

1842 POEMS

When Tennyson did publish again in 1842 a two volume edition entitled *Poems*, he was rewarded for his years of obscure toil. The critics generally agreed that he showed a marked advancement in intellectual depth and technical proficiency. One could say that in 1842 Tennyson as the representative Victorian poet had made his appearance. His interests in the 1842 volumes are wide. Among the most popular when they appeared were the poems of rural domestic life. Such pieces as "Dora," "The Gardener's Daughter," and "The May Queen," to name a few, paint sometimes lovely and sometimes, to modern taste, cloyingly sentimental, idyllic landscapes of English country life.

BREAK, BREAK, BREAK

The new books also contained many short lyrics evoking moods of grey melancholy and quiet despair which characterized Tennyson's earlier volumes. Hallam's death made him feel these moods even more poignantly, and these poems are filled with landscapes of muted colors and sounds which provide a quiet comment on the poet's grief. Tennyson was particularly adept at capturing the various moods of the sea, and his seascapes are some of the most justifiably famous passages in his work.

One of the seascapes most often anthologized is the haunting lyric "Break, Break, Break," in which the poet, without mentioning Hallam, gives expression to a universal sense of loss at the death of a loved one. This sixteen line poem is a good example to study in miniature Tennyson's poetic techniques at their best. Rather than beginning the poem by explicitly mentioning his grief over the loss of a friend, he builds up a mood of quiet despair which makes the final statement of the last **stanza** more powerfully concentrated.

The opening **stanza** describes in a restrained manner the breaking of the waves against the shore:

> **Break, break break,**
> **On thy cold gray stones, O Sea!**
> **And I would that my tongue could utter**
> **The thoughts that arise in me.**

Note the effectiveness of the simple adjectives "cold" and "gray" which contribute an appropriate atmosphere for the emotional state of the speaker. The sea is here not possessed of a radiance or glory of any kind but rather of a harsh, destructive nature. The rhythmical pattern of the first line, with its three heavy stresses and the unaccented stress taken up by the pause between each stressed word, suggests the repetitive beat of the waves as they clash against the rocks. The reiteration of this line to begin **stanza** four, along with the repetition and isolation of the "o" sound five times in the lyric, reinforces the recurring rhythm of the tide.

In the second **stanza** the innocent joy of the fisherman's boy and his sister at play contrasts with the gloomy state of the speaker, who still has not referred to the cause of his sorrow. The **alliteration** of the soft "s" sound ("shouts with his sister") in this **stanza** and throughout the poem is a further example of the sound echoing the sense (onomatopoeia), as it suggests the wind breathing on the shore.

The "stately ships" in **stanza** three which sail on their journey oblivious to the grief of the onlooker, besides painting a pretty picture, suggest that the poet is aware that just as there is joy in the world despite his own feelings, so too the daily business activities of society go on. Only after establishing a scene in which the play of the children, the joy of the sailor, the work of the ships, and even the pounding of the waves suggest a daily pattern of life alien and indifferent to the isolation and loss of the onlooker does Tennyson suggest the situation which gives rise to his emotion:

> But O for the touch of a vanish'd hand,
> And the sound of a voice that is still!

All the sounds which the speaker hears which suggest that the world goes on despite what happens to an individual cannot compensate for the one sound he wants to hear most.

Stanza four is a purposeful variation of stanza one to emphasize that although the speaker realizes that death is a part of the cyclic pattern of life, just as the waves breaking on the shore are part of the repetitive pattern of the sea, yet for him life has been permanently altered by the death of his friend:

Break, break, break,
At the foot of thy crags, O Sea!
But the tender grace of a day that is dead
Will never come back to me.

The sea is an age-old symbol of eternity and mystery because of its vastness and power. It has often been used by poets in contemplating the meaning of life and death. Tennyson in this short poem is therefore not creating any new symbols or attitudes. Rather the poem reveals what a talented poet can do with the commonplace images of daily life when he fuses them into a meaningful unity which helps to convey and substantiate his emotion.

MORTE D'ARTHUR AND THE IDYLLS OF THE KING

Along with the lyrics in the 1842 *Poems* appear two narratives dealing with the Arthurian Legends, most widely known from Thomas Malory's version *Morte d'Arthur* (1485). The first of these poems, "Sir Galahad," is not as successful as Tennyson's retelling of Arthur's death in his own "Morte d'Arthur," which looks forward to the later *Idylls of the King.* Tennyson had long planned to write an **epic** poem on the subject of King Arthur and the Knights of the Round Table, which interestingly enough was the first projected subject of Milton, who later abandoned it for his **epic** *Paradise Lost*. In the 1842 version Tennyson framed the story of the passing of Arthur by a short introduction called "The **Epic**" (lines 1-51) and an epilogue (lines 324-354) describing a party on Christmas Eve in modern times at which a poet reads "Morte d'Arthur" to a circle of friends.

In 1869 Tennyson abandoned his idea of an **epic** poem in favor of a long narrative dealing with the different tales but not as a continuous and integrated narrative. The 1842 "Morte d'Arthur" minus its introduction and epilogue became book XII of the "Idylls." It is interesting to note that the medieval world fascinated Tennyson throughout his life and, as in the case of "In Memoriam", he worked for many years over a subject matter that interested him. Indeed, the last "Idylls" ("Balin and Balan") appeared in 1885, testifying to the poet's lifelong interest in this material.

GREEK MYTHS

Tennyson was also fascinated by the vitality of the Greek myths as poetical subject matter. As in the case of the Arthurian material, this was a lifelong poetic interest. Indeed the 1885 volume in which the last of the "Idylls" appeared had as its title *Tiresias and Other Poems*. The central poem was on the ancient prophet Tiresias who played such an important role in the Oedipus legend.

The **dramatic monologue** "Ulysses" is one of the finest examples of Tennyson's early use of the classical myths. It appeared in the 1842 *Poems*.

DRAMATIC MONOLOGUE

A **dramatic monologue** is a poem in which the personality of one character involved in a dramatic situation is revealed. The character is speaking to an identifiable but silent listener in a critical moment of his life. It is important to note that the speaker in the poem is a creation of the poet, and the thoughts and attitudes he expresses are appropriate to his fictional character and not necessarily identifiable with those of the poet himself. The **dramatic monologue** is an old form but became extremely popular through Robert Browning's extensive use of it. Actually, Tennyson experimented with the form earlier and produced two notable examples in "Tithonus" and the well-known "Ulysses."

ULYSSES

Tennyson's **dramatic monologue** has as its speaker the hero of Homer's *Odyssey*. Ulysses had fought cunningly and bravely to help win victory for the Greeks in the Trojan war. After the war he was forced to wander for ten years through the Mediterranean world with his men, participating in a series of fantastic adventures, before he was finally able to return home to Ithica. Homer ends the tale when Ulysses has returned home, banished his wife's suitors and settled down contentedly to rule his kingdom.

As the monologue opens, Ulysses is an aged man, bored and restless in administering to the routine duties of his pastoral land. After his great years as a leader of men and explorer of the world, he is dissatisfied with the little demand made upon his intelligence and courage in his home. He expresses his determination to set out again to unknown adventures:

> I cannot rest from travel: I will drink
> Life to the lees....(lines 6-7)

It does not matter to the aging warrior that he does not know what danger awaits him or even where he will wander. What is important to him is that he embrace life in all its fullness, whatever it may bring:

> How dull it is to pause, to make an end,
> To rust unburnished, not to shine in use!
> As though to breathe were life. Life piled on life
> Were all too little, and of one to me
> Little remains....(lines 22-26)

So setting off at sunset Ulysses starts on his travels again, unsure of what is ahead, but:

> To strive, to seek, to find, and strong in will not to yield.
> (lines 69-70)

CRITICAL ANALYSIS

What is fascinating about the figure of Ulysses as Tennyson envisions him is that, while clothed in an ancient setting, he is clearly expressing a Tennysonian, and, moreover, a typical Victorian, sentiment. Homer's Ulysses was very anxious to arrive home from his forced travels and once in Ithica expressed no desire to ever leave again. The Greek ideal was moderation; aspiration should never exceed capacity and knowledge. But as Tennyson recreates Ulysses we see that he is using this mythical figure as a symbol to represent the insatiable thirst of man for adventure of every kind; physical, spiritual, and intellectual. What is important is not so much the goal to be reached as the race to be run. This is the positive, attractive side of Tennyson the Victorian spokesman. The side which saw life as a challenge and had unbounded confidence in the ability of man infinitely to progress. This was the Victorian stance which most appealed to Robert Browning, who was more consistent and vigorous in his embracing of life. Tennyson could shout as loudly on occasion as Browning, but sometimes he has the ring of a scared little boy "whistling a happy tuner. This is not obtrusive in "Ulysses" because of the "distancing" or objectifying provided by the mythical framework which distinguishes the emotion from a personal outpouring of feeling on the part of the poet.

Technically the poem is the work of a fine craftsman. Each little detail helps to create a picture in our minds of the scene as Ulysses speaks to his men. The sense of striving as being almost as instinctual and overpowering as a physical need is underscored by the use of imagery connected with the basic physical drives. Note, for example, "drink life to the lees," "roaming with a hungry heart," "drunk delight of battle with my peers." In lines 22-26 (already quoted) notice that Ulysses speaks of a man who refuses to see life as a challenge in terms of a sword which is rusty with disuse and therefore bereft of its beauty and worth. This **metaphor** is further developed when Ulysses speaks of "life piled on life", indicating that a great many lifetimes would still not be enough to satiate his desire to explore, just as a great many bodies piled on a battlefield are not enough to satisfy the warrior until he has achieved complete victory.

The poem is in **blank verse**, which is a stately and vigorous rhythm fit for the stature of a king.

TITHONUS

That Tennyson could not always sustain the mood of optimism and joy in life expressed in "Ulysses" is seen in a companion monologue "Tithonus." Here again the poet uses a classical figure as a symbol. Tithonus was a Trojan prince who received the gift of everlasting life from Aurora, the goddess of the dawn. But in granting her beloved this gift, Aurora neglected to bestow upon him also the gift of everlasting youth. In this **dramatic monologue** Tithonus appears as a very aged man, still dwelling in the palace of the goddess of dawn. But unlike Ulysses, Tithonus prays for death and a release from the unnatural extension of his human life, which, because of its very immortality, is hateful to him. It would not be going too far to assert here that Tennyson is conveying in these two poems the ambiguity which marked his own personality, at times embracing life and at other times fleeing from it.

LOCKSLEY HALL

The 1842 volumes also contained poems dealing with contemporary situations. The most well-known of these is "Locksley Hall." It is concerned with the experience of youth, but it also communicates a protest at the society which sanctions artificial social barriers based on wealth and family and thereby prevents worthy individuals from achieving happiness.

The poem opens with a young soldier bidding his comrades to leave him alone for awhile as they come upon a house very familiar to him, the mansion named Locksley Hall. Alone, the young man recounts in his mind his bitter past experiences with the residents of the house. Using the **convention** of the interior monologue or soliloquy, where the speaker is not actually addressing anyone specifically, but speaking aloud, the young soldier recalls how he first declared his love for his cousin Amy. She reciprocated his feelings for a few happy months. But then Amy, forced by her father's threats, was unfaithful to her promises and instead married a brutish country squire. The soldier bitterly attacks the society which allows women to be completely subjected to men:

> **Cursed be the social wants that sin against the strength of youth!**
> **Cursed be the social lies that warp us from the living truth! (lines 59-60)**

Knowing that he must go on living forever deprived of Amy, the young man ponders what he can do with his life. But his prospects look bleak because bribery and corruption are everywhere. He is barred from advancement due to his lack of money, and even an army career is made dim by the lack of causes for which to fight:

> **But the jingling of the guinea helps the hurt that Honor feels,**
> **And the nations do but murmur, snarling at each others heels.**
> **(lines 105-106)**

Despairing of any hope in England, the young man dreams of seeking refuge from the corruption of society in some faraway Pacific island. He soon realizes, however, that he could never be happy living with people whom he considers his inferiors because they are untouched by the civilization of Western Christian man. At last the dreamer finds consolation in the promise of universal progress guaranteed, he thinks, by the evolutionary principle in

Nature. "Mother Age," the self-determining principle found in Nature, will ensure a brighter future, where society will free itself of its present injustices as it grows spiritually as well as materially. Even though he has become a victim of the present, the young man overcomes his sense of personal tragedy in his confidence in the future of the world:

> **Not in vain the distance beacons. Forward, forward, let us range.**
> **Let the great world spin forever down the ringing grooves of change. (lines 181-182)**

CRITICISM OF LOCKSLEY HALL

This poem is a fascinating period piece. It reveals the tendency of Tennyson, and other Victorian writers, to treat the problem of an individual caught in forces which he cannot control in a manner which robs the work of real tragic stature. Rather than concentrating on the genuine sense of frustration and stifled hopes aroused by the conflict between an individual and the mores of his society, Tennyson is content to castigate society and then undo his protest by announcing his faith in the future. A belief in Darwin's evolutionary theories, as in Tennyson's case, often reenforced the Victorian complacency that somehow things would improve whether man did anything about them or not. This is an extension of the general laissez-faire attitude discussed in the Introduction.

Although "Locksley Hall" is probably autobiographical to a certain extent, it is unwarranted to identify completely, as some critics do, the speaker in the poem with Tennyson himself. The poet claimed that he was trying to portray the attitudes and feelings of youth upon encountering his first major disappointment in life. He stated that the sentiments expressed were not the way he specifically felt while his marriage was delayed due to lack of funds, but the feelings of a typical young man in situation brought about by the false standards of society. The soldier is certainly not an attractive character in his pride and bitterness, and it is rather hard for a modern reader to feel sympathy for his plight when he wishes, at the close of the poem, that a thunderbolt would strike the home of Amy and her family. A certain amount of identification with the author seems justifiable, however, in the comments on society and human progress, since he reiterated them in other poems. It is hard not to laugh today, even allowing for the dramatic situation, over lines which show such an outmoded sense of Christian and English superiority:

> **But I count the gray barbarian lower than the Christian child. (line 174)**
>
> **I, to herd with narrow foreheads, vacant of our glorious gains,**
>
> **Like a beast with lower pleasures, like a beast with lower pains! (lines 175-175)**

"Locksley Hall" is likely to remain a perennial anthology piece despite its obvious defects of overt didacticism and dated ideas. It mirrors the characteristic Tennysonian tension between brooding pessimism over man's nature and faith in the evolutionary process as applied to man's soul as well as to his body. In this poem Tennyson is more insistent, one could almost say bullying, in his belief in progress and his faith that the English were the fittest of the species. While annoying at times, this attitude also contributes a certain vigor and sweep to the poem often absent from his work. The heavily stressed **trochaic** (long-short) foot plus the rhymed **couplets** tend to accentuate the insistent push or movement of the lines.

1847 - THE PRINCESS

With the publication of his next important work "The Princess" Tennyson continued his interest in social reform and committed himself more thoroughly to his role of poet as moralist. This work is actually a versified novelette which preaches the need for greater freedom and education for women. Popular in its day because of its contemporary subject, today it is little read except for the lovely lyrics interspersed throughout the argument. These include the lovely "Tears, Idle Tears," and "Come Down, O Maid."

1850 - SUCCESS ACHIEVED

The great year of both Tennyson's personal and poetic life was 1850. In that year he published his greatest poem "In Memoriam", married Emily Sellwood, and succeeded Wordsworth as poet laureate of England. From this year on his fame was secure, and he went on to become the most popular poet of the second half of the nineteenth century. The longs years of financial distress were at an end, and he purchased a comfortable country house at Blackdown in Surrey, where he lived in security and relative seclusion for his remaining years. After forty-one years of struggling in obscurity, forty-one years of critical renown and continued productivity awaited him.

IN MEMORIAM

This poem is a long (131 sections), unwieldy, and often disunified **elegy** in honor of the poet's friend Arthur Hallam. "In Memoriam" was written over a period of sixteen years, dating from Hallam's death in 1833, in no particular order, and the disparate parts were put together in the late 1830's. The **elegy** has often been criticized as lacking structural harmony. Tennyson usually displays insufficient architectural skill in organizing a lengthy poem, as the *Idylls of the King* testify. The **elegy** does achieve a certain surface unity by using the same stanzaic pattern throughout (abba), but many of the sections are awkwardly linked together and do not make strict progress towards a logical **climax**. Yet it is a mistake to demand too much unity of cohesion from the poem, which is after all an elegy. The elegiac form allows a certain amount of freedom and digression, as witness Milton's "Lycidas" and Shelley's "Adonais." Tennyson's follows the English elegiac tradition, represented in the above poems, in expanding the personal **theme** of grief over the loss of the loved one to a broader consideration of the presence of evil in the world. Like "Lycidas" and "Adonais," "In Memoriam" considers many questions not strictly related to the death of the friend. The nature of the **elegy** demands that the poet probe deeply into the meaning of life, the reason for evil, the validity of religious values, and, usually, the function of art in society. Only after examining these and other questions can the poet hope to find any meaning in death and harmonize his sense of individual loss with the universal pattern of human experience. Because the traditional demands of the elegiac form coincided closely with the questions Tennyson asked himself in his deep grief over Hallam's death, the poet plunged more deeply than usual into the spiritual condition of the Victorian age and is less facile in his conclusions to the conflicts between faith and science, material progress and spiritual deterioration, Christianity and historical research, and other problems tormenting his era.

The sections of the poem vary in mood throughout, and do not consistently proceed along the usual elegiac path of despair, bitterness, contemplation, hope, reconciliation. Tennyson was aware of this alteration in opinions and emotions throughout, but he wanted to communicate a sense of the natural variations in feeling which follow the death of a loved one. The different seasons of the years are skillfully used to form appropriate backdrops for the differing emotions of the poet. In section 11, for example, he describes the ominous calm of an autumn day, which presages the despair upon finally accepting the fact of Hallam's death, with the return of his body to England:

> Calm is the morn without a sound,
> Calm as to suit a calmer grief,
> And only through the faded leaf,
> The Chestnut pattering to the ground; (lines 1-5)

> ....

> Calm and deep peace in this wide air,
> These leaves that redden to the fall,
> And in my heart, if calm at all,
> If any calm, a calm despair. (lines 10-16)

Tennyson's ability to render the sea and the weather in all its aspects, notable in many of his poems, fits in appropriately with the **imagery** of the seasons and the emotions of the poet himself. In section 15, for instance, the storm which follows the calm weather reflects the inner turmoil which comes upon the poet's initial acceptance of Hallam's death:

> Tonight the winds begin to rise
> And roar from yonder dropping day;
> The last red leaf is whirled away,
> The rooks are blown about the skies.
>
> The forest cracked, the waters curled,
> The cattle huddled on the lea;

And wildly dashed on tower and tree
The sunbeam strikes along the world. (lines 1-8)

Although Tennyson's emotions vary along the way, there is a general progress of feeling, through the imaginary time span of the poem of three years, from the different phases of sorrow to tempered joy. His attitude towards the meaning of Christmas (Sections 28, 78, and 104) indicates the stages of his development. The first Christmas after Hallam's death brings him enough hope so that at least he does not wish to join him in death:

This year I slept and woke with pain,
I almost wished no more to wake,
And that my hold on life would break
Before I heard those bells again;

But they my troubled spirit rule,
For they controlled me when a boy;
They bring me sorrow touched with joy,
The merry, merry bells of Yule. (lines 12-20)

By the second Christmas Tennyson has not ceased to grieve, but he has become used to his sorrow and continues to carry on the daily ritual. The third Christmas brings real hope to the poet, who is strengthened by the love of his sweetheart. He ceases to spend his time in fruitless mourning and gathers strength from the very struggle over faith which marked Hallam's life:

Perplexed in faith, but pure in deeds,
At last he beat his music out,
There lives more faith in honest doubt,
Believe me, than in half the creeds. (lines 9-12)

The poet now feels that doubt fought and conquered actually makes a stronger person, and just as Hallam "found a stronger faith his own," so he too will be better because of his victory over the despair death brings. Christmas and the New Year now mean a time of renewed faith for the poet, as he prays that as he overcame his woe so may universal man overcome the sickness in his heart:

Ring in the valiant man and free,
The larger heart, the kindlier hand;
Ring out the darkness of the land,
Ring in the Christ that is to be. (Section 106, lines 29-32)

Significantly with this rebirth of hope comes a renewed joy in nature and the rebirth of Spring:

Where now the seamew pipes, or dives,
In yonder greening gleam, and fly
The happy birds, that change their sky
To build and brood, that live their lives

From land to land; and in my breast
Spring wakens too, and my regret
Becomes an April violet,
And buds and blossoms like the rest (Section 115, lines 13-20)

The over-all direction of the emotional progression of Tennyson from despair to optimism, highlighted by the nature **imagery** and the Christmas passages, is further defined by the descriptions of Hallam's funeral in the beginning of the **elegy**, and the wedding of his sister in the Epilogue. The passages which most appeal to modern readers, however, are those which describe his intense doubt about the afterlife. Sections 54, 55, and 56, for examples, which occur in the mid part of the poem usually are more convincing than the later sections. In Section 55, Tennyson uses the **metaphor** of a man who falls under the weight of a great burden, which echoes Christ's falling under the weight of the cross, to communicate his burden of fear that Christianity may not be valid:

> **I falter where I firmly trod,**
> **And falling with my weight of cares**
> **Upon the great world's altar-stairs**
> **That slope through darkness up to God,**
>
> **I stretch lame hands of faith, and grope,**
> **And gather dust and chaff, and call**
> **To what I feel is Lord of all,**
> **And faintly trust the larger hope. (lines 13-20)**

But after exploring the evolutionary process found in all nature, including the growth of an embryo into a fully developed baby, and listening to the inner promptings of his heart which insist there must be some meaning to life, Tennyson affirms his belief in Christianity and personal salvation. The poet propounds the alliance of religion and scientific evolution, once properly understood. Just as man has progressed from the dumb animals, there is hope that he will continue to evolve spiritually. So too the forms and specific dogmas of Christianity may change, but the spirit of Christ will grow and increase motivating man to rid his society of evil. In the meantime it is the duty of the poet, and every man, to cling to his faith and live by its teachings:

> **With faith that comes of self-control,**
> **The truths that never can be proved**
> **Until we close with all we loved,**

And all we flow from, soul in soul. (Section 131, lines 9-12)

CONCLUSION

1850 marked the height of Tennyson's career, but he remained creative throughout his long life. The canon of his poetry is too extensive to be treated in a general survey. "Ode on the Death of the Duke of Wellington," "Maud," "Enoch Arden," and *The Idylls of the King* are only some of the works which testify to Tennyson's continued productivity until his death. During the 1870's Tennyson tried his hand at writing several poetic dramas. *Queen Mary*, *Harold* and *Becket* are historical plays dealing with the history of England. Four other plays, *The Falcon* (1979), *The Cup* (1881), *The Promise of May* (1892) and *The Foresters* (1892) show little talent on Tennyson's part for the theater. But despite the failure of his plays, the last decade of Tennyson's life was a glorious one. His fame surpassed any of his rivals in England and America. And the poems of his old age, "Rizpah," "To Virgil," "Merlin and the Gleam," are among the best he ever wrote.

THE VICTORIAN POETS

TEXTUAL ANALYSIS

ROBERT BROWNING

The two outstanding poets of the Victorian Period were Tennyson and Browning. Both poets were very much alive to the intellectual and social movements that were so characteristic of their age. It has been generally recognized that Tennyson was the more accomplished poetic craftsman, but that Browning possessed the greater mind. Browning's rich character studies, his intense concern with the complexities of moral order, and his studies of criminal and evil types reveal to us a probing intellect. While Tennyson may well be the poet of richer music and **imagery**, Browning's concern is with matter; he is a poet with something to say, a poet who challenges our minds as we seek to discover the richness of his insight into the vastness of human experience. The psychological insights to be found in Browning's dramatic monologues are proof of the poet's fascination with the varied activities of human intellect and will. His legacy to modern poetry is, as we shall see, a rich one. The modern critical approach to the poem as dramatic utterance is in part due to the particular practice of Robert Browning.

LIFE OF BROWNING

Robert Browning was born in 1812 at Camberwell, a suburb of London. His father was a wealthy businessman who stocked the Browning household with an ample library. His father's love of books, painting, and music was early bestowed upon Robert. With his father, Robert shared an intense interest and love of mysterious tales, and they followed newspaper accounts of fascinating crimes. This last interest may well explain Browning's later attraction to criminal types as subjects of his poems.

Browning's mother reared him according to her beliefs in strict adherence to a code of Evangelical dissent. Robert was a precocious child and he read widely from the extensive library which his home afforded him. His education was not a strictly formal one. Except for brief periods at a boarding school near Camberwell, and later at the University of London, Robert pursued his education within his own home. He received tutoring in foreign languages, music, boxing, and horsemanship. This unusual education gave Robert a rich store of material to draw upon in his poems, and may perhaps explain the excessive obscurity of some of his earlier works.

At the early age of fourteen, Browning read the works of the Romantic poet, Percy Bysshe Shelley. Shelley's early influence led Browning to become an atheist and a liberal (1826). Later Browning left his position of atheism and somewhat modified his early liberal beliefs. However, the influence of Shelley never totally left the poet, for Browning's devotion to ideals and his sense of aspiration toward goals of a lofty nature make him resemble Shelley, though with certain differences. Browning's courtship and marriage to Elizabeth Barrett in 1846 also reveals the romantic side of Browning.

EARLY EFFORTS

Browning's earliest poem "Pauline" appeared anonymously in 1833. In this poem one may notice Browning's early indebtedness to Shelley, for in many ways "Pauline" resembles Shelley's "Alastor". "Pauline" is really an account of Browning's own soul at this young stage in life. He tried to conceal his identity beneath a dramatic framework, but the poem was a failure. Browning later referred to "Pauline" as an "abortion". John Stuart Mill, the nineteenth century philosopher, noted Browning's self-centeredness and morbidness in "Pauline".

PARACELSUS AND SORDELLO

Browning early proposed to himself a "poetry always dramatic in principle", and this was central to his aesthetic. His early failures are landmarks in his effort to achieve the success that was later to be his, particularly in regard to writing dramatic poetry. *Paracelsus* (1835) is a long poetic drama whose central figure is the great Renaissance physician and chemist, Paracelsus. The poem dramatizes the vanity of the protagonist's search for knowledge without love. Aprile, the poet in the poem who symbolizes love as a way of life, sings in the poem of those who fail to use the gifts that God has given them. Sordello (1840) took as its subject the tangled political situation of medieval Italy. In 1838 Browning had visited Italy and he lived there for a great part of his life. Italy was also to provide him the settings of many of his poems. Sordello, however, did great harm to his reputation. While some had greeted the earlier *Paracelsus* as "a marvellous production of youthful genius", Sordello became notorious for its obscurity in subject, style, and treatment.

BROWNING AS DRAMATIST

Elizabethan England had been the high point in dramatic literature, for it was the age of Christopher Marlowe, William Shakespeare, and Ben Jonson. The Romantic Movement of the early nineteenth century sought to emulate the great age of drama. However, nineteenth century drama is singularly disappointing. One thinks, for example, of Tennyson's *Becket*. Browning also tried his hand at drama and was unsuccessful. William Charles Macready, a noted actor of the day, asked Browning to write a play for him. Browning wrote the tragedy *Strafford*. It lasted five performances. Other plays by Browning are *A Blot on the 'Scutcheon*, which resembles *Romeo and Juliet*, *Luria*, and *A Soul's Tragedy*. Browning abandoned the stage, but his failure was not a total disaster. Browning discovered his proper medium in the **dramatic monologue**, and the attempts at playwriting served to shape the poet's powers for later success. The ten years as playwright (1837-47) had been as unsuccessful as some of Browning's early poems had been. Yet he revealed in these early works an ardent idealism and a sharp eye for detached observation of human nature. Along with these Browning also revealed an interest in psychological realities and this, of course, we can see at its best in the dramatic monologues.

BELLS AND POMEGRANATES

From 1841-1846 Browning published eight little pamphlets which were entitled *Bells and Pomegranates*. The first of this series was "Pippa Passes", a fairly lengthy dramatic poem that ultimately became one of Browning's most popular works. Also in this series was *Dramatic Romances and Lyrics* which contained some of Browning's most famous poems including the following: "How They Brought the Good News from Ghent to Aix", "The Flight of the Duchess", the first nine sections of the long poem *Saul*, "The Tomb at St. Praxed's", which was renamed in 1849 "The Bishop Orders His Tomb at St. Praxed's". Five of the pamphlets contained six dramas by Browning. *Dramatic Lyrics* contained two of the outstanding dramatic monologues, "My Last Duchess" and "Soliloquy in a Spanish Cloister".

PIPPA PASSES

This dramatic poem is dated 1841 and is largely a series of rather sordid tales concerned with a young girl named Pippa who is employed in a shop. Pippa works three hundred sixty four days a year and she is on her holiday in the poem. The Introduction reveals Pippa jumping from her bed and celebrating the glories of day. She is free on this day to "play out my fancy's fullest games". Pippa, on this her holiday, is free from her daily chore of winding silk and she pretends that she is in the place of the four happiest people in Asolo, a small Italian town near Venice. Pippa is first Ottima who is involved in adulterous love with Sebald, deceiving her old husband Luca in the process. At lines 114-189 Pippa describes four kinds of love, all belonging to the "happiest four". There is first the illicit passion of Sebald and Ottima which deceives the husband Luca, mentioned above. Secondly there is the innocent conjugal love between Jules and Phrene. The third kind of love is parental love seen between Luigi and his mother. And finally there is religious love in the character of the Bishop (called Monsignor also) who has come to "bless the home/Of his dead brother." The introduction further suggests that Pippa represents the highest type of love-namely the love of God for man.

MORNING

"Pippa Passes" follows the sequence of Pippa's holiday. The first **episode** deals with Ottima and her German lover Sebald whom Pippa discovers conversing about the murder of Luca, Ottima's aged husband. They have already murdered Luca and they now discuss the crime with a view to justifying the deed in light of their present pleasures. However Pippa's song is heard from without:

> **God's in his heaven-**
> **All's right with the world!**

Pippa's song leads Sebald to realize the guilt of his crime and to pronounce his hatred for Ottima.

NOON

In the interval between Morning and Noon, students had tricked the sculptor Jules into marriage. The students discuss their studies-painting and sculpture-with a good deal of **burlesque** humor. Their trick consisted in obtaining a girl, Phrene (Phrene means sea-eagle) to write to Jules that she had been impressed by one of his works. Jules was then to wed her although Phrene was not to speak until they were married. When they were married, Phrene's first speech to Jules was to reveal the trick that had been played on him. The section titled Noon begins with Jules crossing his threshold with his new bride. After Jules describes the interior of his workroom and the sculptures that he has been working on, Phrene reveals her true love for Jules. She also tells Jules of the trick that had been devised by the students. Jules then plans his revenge against the student named Lutwyche, and he decides to allow Lutwyche to live to see a beautiful, finished statue by Jules. It is Pippa's song (lines 253-270) which tells the story of a page who loved far above his station in life that leads Jules to realize the happiness attached to loving a woman "with utter need of me". It is Pippa's song that further makes Jules recognize the futility of revenge.

EVENING

This third **episode** is concerned with the young boy Luigi and his mother. Luigi is an ardent patriot intent on undertaking a dangerous venture in behalf of freedom. Luigi plans to murder a tyrant, but his mother advises against his plan. Luigi though is determined to act to free Italy. Pippa sings a song wherein she describes a virtuous king who prevented a python from assaulting the throne. Luigi now does not waver, for Pippa's song about the virtuous king of olden days confirms in Luigi's mind that "God's voice" calls him to his mission of tyrannicide.

NIGHT

The Bishop comes to Asolo to hear an account of the management of his dead brother's estate by a villainous Intendant, or superintendent. The Intendant has devised a scheme to seduce the rightful heir of the estate and tries to bribe the Bishop. Pippa's song recalls the Bishop from temptation to the true nature of his calling. The Bishop has the Intendant bound and carried off. Pippa's song tells of the love of God. She concludes the poem with the following lines:

> **All service ranks the same with God-**
> **With God, whose puppets, best and worst,**
> **Are we; there is not last nor first.**

"Pippa Passes" thus is an intricate poem treating of critical moments and choices in the lives of several unrelated people. The **episodes** are united by the presence of Pippa whose songs become omens or, as it were, counsels to guide the choices of the characters. She embodies the highest love, and her songs lead the characters to aspire also to a higher form of love. Although Pippa affirms that "God's in his heaven-/ All's right with the world!", the poem indicates quite readily that is not quite so.

PORPHYRIA'S LOVER (1836)

The lover of Porphyria is insane and he is the narrator of this poem, which is an example of Browning's fascination for criminal and evil types as subjects for poetic treatment. The lover tells of Porphyria coming to him and of his realization that "Porphyria worshipped me." The narrator decides to do something, and "all her hair/ In one long yellow string I wound/ Three times her little throat around,/ And strangled her... "The poem is interesting because it is an early example of Browning's use of the poetic monologue. Browning visited Russia in 1834 and is said to have written "Porphyria's Lover" during this trip. The insane lover feels that he has gained a state of permanence by his act, for now Porphyria has shut out all the world: "That all it scorned at once is fled,/ And I, its love, am gained instead!"

Such poems as "Porphyria's Lover" indicate Browning's interest in and his ability to portray villains without overtly condemning them as his Victorian readers had come to expect. Other poems of Browning which reveal a similar attention to the problem of human evil are "The Laboratory" (1844) and "Respectability" (1852).

COUNT GISMOND (1842)

This poem has as its setting Aix in Provence in southern France, and it is written in a six line **stanza** rhyming ababcc. The wife of the Count Gismond speaks to a friend named Adela, and she tells a narrative of the defense of her honor against the accusations of Gautier. The time of the poem is the middle ages which explains the importance of the joust in defense of a woman's honor. Gautier had accused the Queen: "Shall she whose body I embraced/ A night long, queen it in the day?" His charge is levelled as the Queen was about to bestow the tourney prize. Gismond appears to defend her and is victorious over Gautier. Since the duel and its outcome were believed to be acts of providence.

The reader has to put aside suspicion that Gautier spoke truly. The medieval confidence in duels should be noted at lines 70-72 and again at line 83. But the reader must further ask if Gautier was the instrument of the couisins' plot to ruin the character of the Count Gismond's wife. Also, the narrative and dramatic qualities of the poem are deserving of notice - particularly the sharp colloquial and realistic turn in the last **stanza**. Here the speaker abruptly changes subjects upon the entrance of Count Gismond.

HOW THEY BROUGHT THE GOOD NEWS FROM GHENT TO AIX

Browning said that the incident which is told in this poem was imaginary. The poem is a narrative about three riders journeying from Ghent in Belgium to Aix-la Chapelle in West Prussia, a distance of one hundred miles. The town names - Lokeren, Boom, Duffeld, Mecheln, Aershot, Hasselt - which are mentioned in the poem are on the road between the two. One of the outstanding virtues of the poem is the handling of rhythm to suggest the speed of the ride. For example, the use of anapests (two unstressed syllables followed by a stressed syllable) in the first **stanza** quickens the rhythm. The narrator tells of the ride. He is accompanied by Joris and Dirck. The latter two fail to reach Aix because their horses collapse. The speaker, riding his horse Roland, reaches Aix alone with the good news (we are never told what it is), and Roland, the hero, is rewarded with "our last measure of wine".

THE LOST LEADER (1845)

The title refers to William Wordsworth, the great Romantic poet, who as the opening line states: "Just for a handful of silver he left us". Historically the references in the poem are to Wordsworth's acceptance of a government pension in 1842, and the laureatship - "a riband to stock in his coat" - in 1843. In more general terms, the poem is concerned with the loss of a spiritual leader who now "...boasts his quiescence,/ Still bidding crouch whom the rest bade aspire..."

THE BISHOP ORDERS HIS TOMB AT SAINT PRAXED'S CHURCH

John Ruskin, nineteenth century essayist and critic, in his *Stones of Venice* said that he knew "of no other piece of modern English prose or poetry, in which there is so much told, as in these lines, of the Renaissance spirit, - its worldliness, inconsistency, pride, hypocrisy, ignorance of itself, love of art, of luxury, and of good Latin." The poem, however, is centrally concerned with a man first and secondarily with a Renaissance Bishop. It is not simply a period piece. Browning wrote a number of poems whose subjects were derived from the Italian Renaissance, and one must remember that Browning lived a good part of his life in Italy and was very fond of medieval and Renaissance subjects. In this particular poem, Browning presents a very human portrait of a churchman who is more concerned with the quality of the marble for his tombstone than with thoughts of the hereafter. The poem thus takes as its setting a time when corruption existed in ecclesiastical circles and when reformers such as Erasmus were crying out for reform. Yet the reader should concentrate attention upon the character portrait of the Bishop rather than attempt to read the poem as historical comment. "The Bishop Orders His Tomb", written in 1845, gives us an instance of Browning's skillful use of the **dramatic monologue** form.

"The Bishop Orders His Tomb" is a monologue in **blank verse** (unrhymed iambic **pentameter**), spoken by the Bishop to his illegitimate sons, who are euphemistically called "Nephews - sons mine" (line 3). The poem opens: "Vanity, saith the preacher, vanity!", a quote from Ecclesiastes 1:2, and the entire poem has to do with this text. One meets vanity in the character of the worldly Bishop as he tells his sons of the envy of Gandolf, his predecessor as bishop, for their mother. The Bishop, now on his death-bed, is tossed between thoughts of life and death and he seeks the meaning of each. He asks "Do I live, am I dead?", and he repeats the question at line 113 indicating that his mind is wandering and that he is uncertain whether he is damned or saved. At line 17 he tells that Gandolf cozened him by selecting a choice spot for his grave, but the Bishop is determined to erect an elaborate tomb which the dead Gandolf will envy:

Old Gandolf with his paltry onion-stone,
Put me where I may look at him! True peach,

> Rosy and flawless: how I earned the prize!
> (lines 31-33)

Lines 34ff. relate how the Bishop planned to say that he had saved the lapis lazuli (an azure blue, opaque, semi-precious stone) if it had been missed after a conflagration of his church. The stone was not missed, and so the Bishop buried it for personal use at a later time. He now tells his sons to dig it up from the "white-grape vineyard where the oil press stood." This, along with the design which the Bishop requests for the tomb, reveals the conscience and the character of the wordly cleric. The mixture of pagan and Christian elements for the design reveals his divided nature. Fearing lest his sons fail to provide for his sumptuous tomb, the Bishop reminds them that he is leaving them a considerable inheritance:

> And have I not Saint Praxed's ear to pray
> Horses for ye, and brown Greek manuscripts,
> And mistresses with great smooth marbly limbs?
> (lines 73-75)

The Bishop then requests that his **epitaph** be in the "choice Latin" of Tully, rather than in the inferior Latin of Ulpian which adorns the tomb of Gandolf. He dismisses his sons, noting their ingratitude, and asks that they leave him in death in the peace of his church:

> That I may watch at leisure if he leers-
> Old Gandolf- at me, from his onion-stone,
> As still he envied me, so fair she was!
> (lines 123-125)

Thus we note in the final words of the Bishop the direct, realistic, and colloquial tone achieved by Browning in this poem. The Bishop has revealed his character to us at a decisive moment - the moment of death. However, the poem does not really invite explicit moral condemnation of the Bishop. Perhaps better we should note the **irony** involved in the Bishop's self-revelation, an **irony** which confirms his own judgment: "Evil and brief hath been my pilgrimage." At times the Bishop delights the reader, and at other times he would seem to call for moral reproof. Perhaps, in the end, it would be best to think of the Bishop as a character who has laid bare his soul, and we, the readers, have seen the tensions that exist within a man who is perchance all too human.

MARRIAGE TO ELIZABETH BARRETT

Elizabeth Barrett was a famous poetess when Robert Browning met her in 1845. Elizabeth was six years older than Robert and she was a semi-invalid. Her father was a very possessive parent who objected strenuously to any relationship with Browning. The romance between Robert and Elizabeth had many of the romantic earmarks that were so loved by Browning. Robert was forced to visit Elizabeth by secret arrangement so that he might avoid the ill will of her father. Ultimately they eloped on Sept. 12, 1846 despite her father's opposition. Elizabeth's father never forgave her for what she had done. However, Robert and Elizabeth were married and they settled at Casa Guidi in Italy where they lived from 1847-1861. After their marriage, Elizabeth's health improved greatly, and they were both able to live a full and happy life together. A son was born to them to share their happiness. Elizabeth was interested in Italian politics while Robert was "attracted to Italian painting, history, and music. During the years of marriage, Browning wrote one of his greatest volumes of poetry *Men and Women* (1855). Mrs. Browning died in 1861, and Robert returned to London with his son.

DRAMATIC MONOLOGUES

As a literary form the **dramatic monologue** is an especially fine and unique form of expression. It combines lyric and drama, and in it one finds the poet impersonating another character, who may be historical or fictitious. When one thinks of the type, such poems as Tennyson's "Ulysses," T. S. Eliot's "Gerontion" and "The Love Song of J. Alfred Prufrock," and of course the magnificent monologues of Robert Browning come to mind. In our own century the poetry of T. S. Eliot has reiterated the dramatic nature of lyric verse. Yet this same dramatic quality may be found in the poems of the seventeenth century poets John Donne and George Herbert. It would be hard to deny that Donne's "The Canonization" is a dramatic poem as well as Herbert's "The Collar." Indeed by extension the term dramatic may also be applied to the **sonnets** of Shakespeare. Thus in many ways to see lyric verse as essentially dramatic is a practice of modern criticism.

Yet one needs a working vocabulary which will enable him to examine the dramatic qualities of Browning's poems. In the **dramatic monologue** a speaker is heard addressing a second person. Although the second person may be well defined by the poet, he does not enter the action but serves as audience for the speaker. The reader, as it were, looks on as the speaker converses with the hearer. As in drama, so too in the **dramatic monologue** we find action of a significant nature which is structured along the lines of a beginning, middle, and end. The action which occurs happens in the present, so that the monologue differs from dramatic narrative which relates past events. However, the chief concern of the **dramatic monologue** is character and not action. It is a form particularly suited to reveal the hidden motives for choices and actions. Thus we discover a character confronted by a critical situation and we learn the motives of the character for the particular action which he takes. Therefore the **dramatic monologue** is a form particularly appropriate to reveal the inner recesses of the soul at a moment of crucial choice.

MY LAST DUCHESS

Browning, as we have seen, early espoused for himself an aesthetic that called for a poetry essentially dramatic. Some of the poems already examined revealed dramatic qualities, but with the publication of *Dramatic Lyrics* (1842), Browning brought forth some of his best work, much of it in the **dramatic monologue** form. "My Last Duchess" is a dramatic monologue which reveals the character of a Duke who has had his Duchess murdered because he refused to stoop to correct her flirtatious, plebeian ways. The Duke addresses a listener whose presence is very definitely felt and he relates the events and reasons for his action as regards the Duchess.

The Duke appears on the surface to be a cold-hearted tyrant who has destroyed his Duchess. The Duke speaks to the visiting envoy of the Count, and he shows the envoy a portrait of his Duchess painted by Fra Pandolf. We come to know the Duchess from what the Duke says of her, and she appears to have been flirtatious and not too careful to please her husband:

> **She had**
> **A heart- how shall I say? - too soon made glad,**
> **Too easily impressed; she liked whate'er**
> **She looked on, and her looks went everywhere.**

The Duke is proud and jealous. He refused to remonstrate with the Duchess: "I choose never to stoop." The Duchess had smiled too much for the Duke. Throughout the poem, the Duke speaks in a quiet, ironic tone, and such remarks as a "officious fool," and his descent of the staircase reveal him to us. He was hurt because his wife found no pride in a nine hundred year old name which he considered a great gift to her. The abrupt ending on the staircase with the envoy, and the Duke's descent alongside the envoy rather than before him lend an ironic note. At the end we find the Duke turning his attention away from the portrait of his Duchess to the more immediate concerns of the marriage to the Count's daughter. The conversational tone of the closing lines is revealing:

> Nay, we'll go
> Together down, sir! Notice Neptune, though,
> Taming a sea-horse, thought a rarity,
> Which Claus of Innsbruck cast in bronze for me!

Here the dramatic tone is apparent, and further we note that the Duke who refused to stoop with his wife could defer to others. The matter-of-fact manner of the Duke discussing the paintings on the wall is also important to consider, for we must remember that he has just had his wife murdered. Although it is not specifically stated in the poem that the Duchess had been murdered, Browning himself said that "the commands were that she should be put to death, or he might have had her shut up in a convent." Again the reader is not invited to judge the Duke too quickly as a proud, avaricious, and villainous tyrant. Browning often did not satisfy his Victorian audience in their quest for an obvious moral, and "My Last Duchess" would seem to point out that the Duke is not a total villain nor is the Duchess all saint. It first appeared in the collection of 1842 titled *Dramatic Lyrics*.

SOLILOQUY IN THE SPANISH CLOISTER

Like "My Last Duchess" this dramatic monologue also appeared in the 1842 collection *Dramatic Lyrics*. It has been generally assumed that this monologue presents a brilliant study of the intense passion of hate within the seemingly placid confines of a monastery. The narrator is a monk who speaks to us of his loathing for a fellow monk, Brother Lawrence, a genuine bore. Brother Lawrence is portrayed as an extremely punctillious type who is particularly annoying to the speaker.

> Gr-r-r- there go, my heart's abhorrence!
> Water your damned flower-pots, do!
> If hate killed men, Brother Lawrence,
> God's blood, would not mine kill you!

The opening lines of the poem indicate the colloquial tone and the feelings of the speaker toward Brother Lawrence. The excessive care with which Brother Lawrence tends his flowers, his boring conversation at table, and his failure to practice the religious observances of the speaker all lead to detestation. Hatred is not though the real emotion or concern of the poem, but petty spite or envy of a person whose every move annoys us. Consider for example lines 45-48:

> How go on your flowers? None double?
> Not one fruit-sort can you spy?
> Strange! - And I, too, at such trouble
> Keep them close-nipped on the sly!

At lines 49-70 we see the speaker's fancy at play in an ingenious, half-amused way as he quotes texts from Galatians, mentions the Manichean heresy, and a possible contract with the devil for Brother Lawrence's soul. At the conclusion the bells call the speaker to vespers and away from watching the loathed movements of Brother Lawrence. His last line: "Ave, Virgo! Gr-r-r- you swine!" juxtaposes the religious setting and recalls the opening line of the poem and the study of human envy and spite. Thus we have discovered a man's soul as regards another man. "Soliloquy in a Spanish Cloister" reveals the speaker's intense dislike for Brother Lawrence, a dislike in part caused by the kind of bore that the Brother is.

FRA LIPPO LIPPI

Browning took as his subject for this poem the fifteenth century painter Lippo Lippi and he based his account on a reading of Vasari's *Lives of the Painters*. The poem first appeared in the 1855 collection *Men and Women*. The poem opens with the escape of Fra Lippo from his monastery and his apprehension by the night watch. Lippo addresses the guard and persuades them to unhand him. He asks: "Who am I?" and answers his own question by informing the guard that he is in the service of Cosimo of the Medici (1389-1464), a patron of the arts and the real ruler of Florence. The mention of Cosimo's name forces the guards to release their hold on Lippo's throat. With his painter's eye he notices one of the guards fit for a painting: "He's Judas to a tittle, that man is!" Another of the guards he finds suited for the slave holding the head of John the Baptist. He invites the captain to sit so that he may explain why they have caught him "at an alley's end/ Where sportive ladies leave their doors ajar?", and also that he may reveal his life's story. Lippo had been painting saints for his patron for three weeks when he leaned out the window for fresh air and spied some young ladies sporting in the evening air. Here he appeals to the guard's spirit of licentiousness- "zooks, sir, flesh and blood,/ That's all I'm made of!" and describes how he tied knots in his coverlet to escape Cosimo's house. After he had his fun "Hard by Saint Laurence", he began his way back to the house but was apprehended by the guard. Lippo says that he sought some sleep before beginning his portrait of St. Jerome. The contrast between the saint and the painter sets up an ironic contrast of the habits of the two men.

At line 80 Lippo begins an account of his youth. One notes, of course, that Lippo constitutes the speaker and the "you" or captain of the guards is his audience. The story of his youth is that of a gamin who became a monk and then a painter. Left in the street as a child, Lippo was taken to a convent and accepted as a monk:

> **Brief, they made a monk of me;**
> **I did renounce the world, its pride and greed,**
> **Palace, farm, villa, shop, and banking house,**
> **Trash, such as these poor devils of Medici**
> **Have given their hearts to- all at eight years old.**
> **(lines 97-101)**

Lippo found that the life of the monastery afforded him a life of ease and idleness which he had never known. Unable to learn Latin, he took to drawing in his copy-books and in the margin of his antiphonary, or choir book. His experience as a gamin had given him a rich education and knowledge of human faces and personalities. This talent gives Lippo the task of painting in the monastery and his work is greeted with disapproval. His saints and angels have the faces of the many humans whom Lippo saw as a boy in the streets. His **realism** is at first greeted as follows:

> **"That's the very man!**
> **Look at the boy who stoops to pat the dog!**
> **That woman's like the Prior's niece who comes**

To care about his asthma: it's the life!"
(lines 168-171)

This enthusiastic reaction of certain of the monks is soon tempered, however, by the superiors who refuse to approve Lippo's realistic technique. Lippo's work is branded "devil's game," and they advise Lippo to imitate the example of Giotto (1276-1337). The following is the aesthetic credo opposed to Lippo's conception of art:

> Your business is not to catch men with show,
> With homage to the perishable clay,
> But lift them over it, ignore it all,
> Make them forget there's such a thing as flesh.
> (lines 179-182)

Lippo is told that it is his job "to paint the souls of men" and "never mind the legs and arms!" This theory is alien, however, to the aesthetic **realism** of Lippo who sees beauty in the reality of things and people drawn exactly from life. He pronounces his theory of art at lines 215-220:

> Or say there's beauty with no soul at all-
> (I never saw it- put the case the same-)
> If you get simple beauty and naught else,
> You get about the best thing God invents:
> That's somewhat: and you'll find the soul you have missed.
> Within yourself, when you return him thanks.

Lippo is convinced of the value of human flesh, and he firmly believes that the infinite variety of life is not to be passed over in an attempt to ignore it, but instead it is to be wondered at in its beauty. Painting should call our attention to the significance of the everyday events that we may pass without noting their importance and beauty:

> **This world's no blot for us,**
> **Nor blank; it means intensely, and means good:**
> **To find its meaning is my meat and drink.**
> **(lines 313-315)**

Browning himself greatly admired the figure of Lippo for opposing the artistic tendencies of his times. Browning felt that he too, like Lippo, offered a certain **realism** opposed to the idealism and optimism of his age. In his complex character studies wherein judgement is suspended, we can see that Browning succeeded. Lippo rejects (see lines 315 ff.) **didactic** theories of art, and maintains a position more nearly that of "art for art's sake". He concludes with an elaborate description of his painting "The Coronation of the Virgin" for St. Ambrose's Church. The painting includes Lippo himself in the lower right hand corner led into the august company by St. Lucy, who is painted with the face of the Prior's niece (see lines 170, 195-6, 208-9). This marks a triumph for Lippo, the "monk out of bounds", and he concludes with the colloquial lines to the captain: "The street's hushed, and I know my own way back,/ Don't fear me! There's the grey beginning. Zooks!" In this monologue we do not really come to know Lippo as a man, but instead we learn of him as artist and are made aware of the debate between conflicting theories. In large part it is a narrative defense of the practice of Lippo. However, there is a dramatic moment - the seizure by the guards - and Lippo seizes this to expound his views and to narrate his history. The fact that he has been seized while out of his monastery is subsumed beneath the primary concern of the poem, namely the **exposition** of a theory of art with which Browning held great sympathy. Yet one should notice the human elements in the portrait and also the skillful handling of dialogue and character. It is certainly one of Browning's best dramatic monologues.

ANDREA DEL SARTO

This monologue is an almost perfect example of the type and may well be Browning's finest. It first appeared in the collection *Men and Women* (1855), and Browning wrote the poem in response to a request from his munificent benefactor John Kenyon. Kenyon had asked Browning for a photographic reproduction of Andrea del Sarto's portrait of himself with his wife which hung in the Pitti Palace, Florence. Browning was unable to find a reproduction and so composed and sent the poem to Kenyon. Again as in "Fra Lippo Lippi" Browning used Vasari's *Lives of the Painters* for details concerning the life of the Florentine painter who lived from 1486-1531. Andrea was a painter famed for his technical skill but one lacking the artistic gifts of true inspiration, grandeur, and genius. The poem thus becomes a study of "failure in success", and the reader should consider it with its complement "The Last Ride Together", a study of success in failure. When reading Vasari, Browning's mind seized on the following statement about Andrea del Sarto: "there was a certain timidity of mind, a sort of diffidence and want of force in his nature." Building on this, Browning wrote his penetrating study of a character whom we would generally call pathetically weak.

Andrea is a man of considerable talent who has married an ignorant wife, Lucrezia. She is in large part responsible for his failure to reach the pinnacle of greatness in art. The poem opens as Andrea speaks to Lucrezia: "But do not let us quarrel any more,/ No, my Lucrezia; bear with me for once;/ Sit down and all shall happen as you wish." The tone of address immediately informs us that Andrea is a victim of the destructive influence which Lucrezia wields over him. Throughout the poem we are increasingly made aware of the tragic aspects of Andrea's character, for the poem is his moment of self-revelation. It is evening and Andrea and Lucrezia sit together looking at the view of Fiesole, a suburb of Florence, from their window. She serves as the model for Andrea; however, she is totally disinterested in his work and is instead a financial burden. The **imagery** of color that Browning uses throughout is suggestive of the character of Andrea and of his art. Silver-grey, autumn, and twilight are contrasted to the gold of Michaelangelo and Raphael. The ironic tone to the symbol of Lucrezia's "golden hair" also adds much to the total effect. Gold is used in the literal sense of money (see lines 217-218). The association of autumn with Andrea is evident at lines 45-51:

> **And autumn grows, autumn in everything.**
> **Eh? the whole seems to fall into a shape**
> **As if I saw alike my work and self**
> **And all that I was born to be and do,**
> **A twilight-piece. Love, we are in God's hand.**
> **How strange now, looks the life he makes us lead;**
> **So free we seem, so fettered fast we are!**

Note in the last line of the quotation the balance and the effective use of "seem" and "are", the contrast of appearance and reality. Lucrezia is unable to understand Andrea's art nor does she care to try to understand. Yet he is an accomplished craftsman who no longer needs to sketch outlines. Indeed his talents are those which others might envy. But Andrea is judged and the paintings of Michaelangelo and Raphael are much superior: "...I am judged./ There burns a truer light of God in them,/ In their vexed beating stuffed and stopped-up brain" (lines 78-80). Browning himself thought of life as a moral testing ground and admired heroic aspiration. Andrea, though, is a painter whose aspirations are not high and he reveals his self-awareness in lines 97-99:

> **Ah, but a man's reach should exceed his grasp,**
> **Or what's a heaven for? all is silver-grey**
> **Placid and perfect with my art: the worse!**

"Andrea Del Sarto" is a poem of acquiescence, and the language is used effectively to create a mood of calm, of failure in success. The poem is enveloped by the very same silver-grey mist that is the background of Andrea's paintings. His technical mastery is indicated as he looks about his room and sees a painting by Raphael with an arm out of perspective. Yet Andrea is aware that the soul in Raphael is right. Lucrezia had failed in not bringing soul and mind to Andrea to assist him in his work. Then he recalls his work for King Francis I of France and how he misused money given him by the King to buy paintings. Andrea instead used the money to build a house for himself and Lucrezia. This conversion of gold into something to please Lucrezia rather than into art is symbolic of his career. Andrea recalls his "kingly days", and he speaks of his sometime glory: "I surely then could sometimes leave the ground,/ Put on the glory, Rafael's daily wear". But Andrea turns to Lucrezia and recognizes the fate he has chosen for himself - one of subservience to Lucrezia - "You called me, and I came home to your heart." At the conclusion Lucrezia's lover enters, and Andrea resigns himself to the fact that he must sit alone through the evening:

> **Only let me sit**
> **The grey remainder of the evening out,**
> **Idle, you call it, and muse perfectly**
> **How I could paint, were I but back in France,**
> **One picture, just one more - the Virgin's face,**

> Not yours this time! I want you at my side
> To hear them - that is, Michel
> Agnolo - Judge all I do and tell you of its worth.
> (lines 226-223)

Andrea, however, turns away from this moment of self-bemused aspiration and recognizes the reality of his situation and of his choice. He agrees to finish the portraits for Lucrezia's friend and this may pay "for this same Cousin's freak" (cousin here means lover). Thus "Andrea del Sarto" reveals the soul of a weak man who has married a woman of great physical beauty. Lucrezia, like the paintings of Andrea, is of great form but she is without soul. The pleading tone of Andrea as he asks her not to treat him so badly reveals his character to us. Yet we have caught Andrea in a moment of self-awareness and we see the yawning chasm that exists between aspiration and achievement. The final lines of the poem reveal the ideal which Andrea would aspire to and the reality of his situation, a situation which he has created and is unable to escape from:

> In heaven, perhaps, new chances, one more chance-
> Four great walls in the New Jerusalem,
> Meted on each side by the angel's reed,
> For Leonard, Rafael, Agnolo and me
> To cover - the three first without a wife,
> While I have mine! So - still they overcome
> Because there's still Lucrezia, - as I choose.
> (lines 260-266)

THE LAST RIDE TOGETHER

This poem reveals the characteristic dramatic quality of Browning and treats the success in failure **theme**. It is also a noteworthy expression of one Browning's favorite themes, namely the superiority of love over glory and art. In this poem the speaker rejects all for the moment which he seeks to make eternal, and this moment is the beauty of love. The speaker finds importance in "The instant made eternity", and at the close of the poem rides off with his sweetheart. By all accounts, though, this is a relatively shallow poem with its celebration of all that is "romantic" in a derogatory sense of the word. The attempt to make the human passion of love the highest goal of aspiration on Browning's part is not quite convincing, and it is rather strange to find a poet denigrating the importance of art as we find Browning doing in this poem. One of the merits of "The Last Ride Together" is the suggestive handling of rhythm which approximates the idea of the ride.

CHILDE ROLAND TO THE DARK TOWER CAME

This poem also first appeared in the 1855 collection *Men and Women*. Browning wrote "Childe Roland" in January 1852 in a single day, and the poem is more fantasy and dream-like than the characteristic intellectual bent of the majority of Browning's work. The title of the poem is taken from Shakespeare's *King Lear* (III, iv, 187-190) and Edgar's speech. In Shakespeare's play the aged king is about to enter a hovel on the heath and Edgar, feigning madness, utters the following lines which recall the quests and challenges of fairy tales: "Child Rowland to the dark tower came;/ His word was still/ 'Fie, foh, and fum!/ I smell the blood of a British man!" The word "childe" in the title must be understood in the sense of a youth of gentle birth and usually a youth who is a candidate for knighthood.

Childe Roland is on a quest in the poem and he meets a "hoary cripple" from whom he seeks direction to the Dark Tower. Roland is aware of the apparent failure of his search and he notes the glee with which the "hateful cripple" points him on his way. Roland had "so long suffered in this quest" that he wishes now only to be worthy of the attempt as others before him had been. The plain over which Roland rides is one of utter dreariness and desolation. He sees a horse on the plain: "Seldom went such grotesqueness with such woe;/ I never saw a brute I hated so;/ He must be wicked to deserve such pain." Later a little river crossed his path and again the presentation of bleakness, suffering, and decay continues. At last the plain gives way to the sight of mountains, and Roland sees the Dark Tower in their midst. His mysterious journey at an end, Roland sees the round, squat tower and those who have gone before him and failed. The lost adventurers of before seem to form a living frame to enclose the failure of Roland. Yet Roland is dauntless and faithful to the ideal which started him on his quest. With courage in the face of failure Roland recognizes all who have gone before him and announces his arrival: "Dauntless the slug-horn to my lips I set,/ and blew. 'Childe Roland to the Dark Tower came.'" The poem is written in six line **stanzas** which **rhyme** abbaab. Interpretations of the mystery of the Dark Tower have often led to allegorical readings. However, Browning indicated that he had no allegorical intention in writing the poem, and he once agreed that the following statement offered by a friend might sum up the meaning of "Childe Roland": "He that endureth to the end shall be saved." No matter what allegorical meaning we may feel the context sustains, it would seem that the **imagery**, mood, and tone of "Child Roland" point to the feeling of despair and resignation in the face of a struggle man must undertake. In this way it is akin to T. S. Eliot's "Hollow Men". But other readers find that the poem expresses courage and defiance. Thus the student can see that poetry cannot be reduced to a simple prose meaning, but instead may sustain several interpretations provided they are based on a close reading of the text.

A GRAMMARIAN'S FUNERAL

This poem, also appearing in 1855, celebrates the Renaissance thirst for learning and knowledge in the character of a dead scholar whose corpse is carried by his students. The speaker of the poem is one of the dead grammarian's former students. The student utters a defense of his former master's idealistic pursuit of learning and knowledge and his faith in the future life. The speech of the student juxtaposes the ideals of the scholar against the petty realities of worldly life, and the poem has often been noted for its harsh-sounding and laborious verse. The scholar, however, becomes a kind of hero whose devotion to grammar has enabled others in the Renaissance to pursue learning all the more easily. In another poem "Sibrandus Schafnaburgensis" Browning ridiculed pedantry, but here learning is held up as a lofty ideal.

BROWNING'S LATER LIFE AND DEATH

After the death of Mrs. Browning, Browning returned to London with his son. The publication of Dramatis Personae in 1864 indicated a marked turn of attention from Italian to English **themes** and also a notable interest in topics of the day. "Caliban Upon Setebos", for example, revealed Browning's interest in current controversies. In this poem two important controversies of the Victorian period are examined, namely the Darwinian hypothesis concerning evolution and secondly the controversy concerning the existence of God which had been excited during the period by Biblical Higher Criticism. The title of this poem means Caliban's thoughts about Setebos. Caliban, the earth creature, half-monster and half-man, is taken by Browning from Shakespeare's *The Tempest*, and through his speech in the poem we see the kind of theology formed by primitive man who fashions his idea of God from the observation of natural phenomena and not from divine revelation. Caliban's idea of God is that of a willful creature of great power. Also during this period Browning turned to grotesque subjects as may be seen in the poem "A Death in the Desert".

THE RING AND THE BOOK

This lengthy poem was published in installments from 1868-1869, and Browning's success with this work ranked him with Tennyson as one of the most popular poets of the period. *The Ring and the Book* is a series of **dramatic monologues** in twelve books, and though its length is formidable the serious and advanced student of Browning cannot neglect it. The story of the poem is based on an old murder trial dating from 1698 in Florence. In 1860 Browning had discovered on a Florentine bookstall the "Old Yellow Book" which contained a collection of records of an old murder trial as well as an account of the execution of the accused party. Browning based his lengthy masterpiece on this account. In the poem we come to know the characters and the motivations for their actions in connection with this old event.

THE STORY

Pompilia, the adopted daughter of Pietro Comparini, an old Roman, married Guido Franceschini, but the girl fled from her husband and returned to Rome in the company of Giuseppe Caponsacchi, a priest. Guido, however, followed after and murdered Pompilia's parents and left Pompilia fatally wounded. The background of Pompilia's adoption leads some of the people to lay blame with Violante, the mother, who bought

THE VICTORIAN POETS

Pompilia from a prostitute but deceived her husband, Pietro, into believing that she was a legitimate child of her own. Other details of Pompilia's association with Caponsacchi are provided, and this further leads some to sympathize with Guido. Others, though, sympathize with Pompilia, and believe that she was the victim of Guido. Guido tells his story of poverty, of his marriage to Pompilia for her dowry in exchange for his noble name, of the fact that his brothers are priests, and of Pompilia's failure as a wife. He tells that she spied Caponsacchi at the opera, and later through devious means arranged meetings with her lover. Pompilia's child is not his, Guido states. In all Guido lists the many grievances which he feels justified his crime of passion and he throws himself upon the mercy of the court. Caponsacchi comes to the stand and tells how Pompilia sought his help and that the letters between him and Pompilia were forgeries. He adds that the account of the dying Pompilia confirms the fact that all was a plot contrived by Guido. The Pope pronounces Pompilia innocent in one of the best of the books in the poem. Finally, Guido and his accomplices are hanged despite Guido's plea for mercy.

BROWNING AND LADY ASHBURTON

As indicated in the discussion of Browning's marriage to Elizabeth Barrett, theirs was a happy life together. Recalling his love and devotion to Elizabeth, Robert made a rather half-hearted proposal of marriage to Lady Ashburton in 1871. However, Browning proposed with such undying loyalty to his former wife that Lady Ashburton could do nothing but refuse. A previous incident regarding Elizabeth might be mentioned in this connection to illustrate Robert's devotion to Elizabeth. In 1861 the Victorian poet Edward FitzGerald had written to a friend on the death of Mrs. Browning: "Mrs. Browning's death is rather a relief to me, I must say: no more Aurora Leighs (title of one of her poems), thank God!... She and her sex had better mind the kitchen and the children." Browning was very angered when he discovered this and published a sharp retort "To Edward FitzGerald" in the Athenaeum: "Kicking you seems the common lot of curs -/ While more appropriate greeting lends you grace,/ Surely to spit there glorifies your-face-/ Spitting from lips once sanctified by hers." Browning never married again, but he continued a working and productive poet until his death in 1889. Browning died at a time when his popularity had reached great heights. He was buried in Westminster Abbey.

RABBI BEN EZRA

The speaker in this poem is Abraham Ibn Ezra (ca. 1092-1167), who was an eminent Biblical scholar of Spain. The poem is not dramatic but declamatory in its presentation of Ibn's thought which is colored by optimism and idealism. Browning, although he used the historical figure of Ibn, did not try to re-create the philosophy or spirit of the medieval thinker. Critics have often, perhaps too closely, identified the thought of this poem with Browning's thought. The poem speaks of the advance of age and the decline of youth, and a philosophy of joyous acceptance is offered. Man is pictured as creature of flesh and soul, both glorious and important. Trust in God is offered despite the inability of man to achieve what he aspires to. The glory of aspiration is again celebrated: "Shall life succeed in that it seems to fail:/ What I aspired to be,/ And was not comforts me:/ A brute I might have been, but would not sink i' the scale." The hedonistic philosophy of Edward FitzGerald's *Rubaiyat of Omar Khayyam* is rejected in "Rabbi Ben Ezra", and age is looked upon as a maturing process which prepares man for his "adventure brave and new" - that of eternal life. The elaborate **metaphor** of the potter's wheel and of the clay vessel at the end of the poem indicate that man's task on earth is one of preparation for his end with God - "to slake Thy thirst". The poem concludes: "Perfect the cup as planned!/ Let age approve of youth, and death complete the same!"

CONCLUSION AND COMMENT

The career of Robert Browning is one that begins with the failures of youthful efforts and concludes with the successes of the accomplished and recognized poet. In the 1860's Browning came to be recognized along with Tennyson as the outstanding figures in poetry of the Victorian Period. Some readers have looked to Browning's work as a kind of moral tonic, pointing no doubt to poems that celebrate the glory of human aspiration and courage. Thus the formation of Browning Societies was undoubtedly stimulated by the fact that readers felt that Browning offered them religious teaching and a code of optimism in place of the doubt and uncertainty so characteristic of Tennyson and Arnold. The following lines from "Prospice", which is concerned with the approach of death, lend themselves to this kind of response by readers:

> I was ever a fighter, so - one fight more,
> The best and the last!
> I would hate that death bandaged my eyes, and forbore,
> And bade me creep past.
> No let me taste the whole of it, fare like my peers
> The heroes of old,
> Bear the brunt, in a minute pay glad life's arrears
> Of pain, darkness and cold.

A second group of readers, however, would not read Browning for his solution of problems of doubt but instead for his attempts to work with the problem of how poetry should be written. Thus the handling of rhythm, language, image, and treatment of poetic subject would particularly interest this group. The complexities of the dramatic monologues, for instance, allow no simple answers as to how one should look at the characters treated at moments of critical choice and action. Indeed Browning may well be asking that we not make moral decisions but behold the range of human passion, thought, and action.

At times there is obscurity and difficulty of **syntax** in Browning's verse, and such ideas as the doctrine of love as a process of "elected affinities" may well seem silly to us. The latter notion is one that involves a romantic elevation of love into a form of spiritual inspiration and may be seen in "The Last Ride Together". Despite these faults, Browning is an important poet, one who for all practical purposes established the **dramatic monologue** as a standard for modern poetry. Poetry to Browning was a serious matter and his chief concern is not with pure nature but with human action. He is concerned with the realities of everyday life and with men acting in human society. His aesthetic credo, which postulated that his poetry would be essentially dramatic, indicates this interest in human action and motivation. There is, of course, an obvious **didactic** strain in Browning, and some readers have felt that his ethical and religious views are shallow. Yet one must take into account the age of skepticism in which he wrote. Browning acutely felt the clash between faith and reason and he choose to emphasize love and faith. Thus there is pity and understanding in his portraits of apparently evil characters - a feeling that there will be a brighter horizon. Browning's optimism then is really a religious optimism. Reason for Browning was insufficient to solve the problems of sin and doubt that beset his age, and thus he turned to love. Browning further thought of life as a kind of moral proving-ground wherein faith is tested and thus his repeated emphasis upon the glory of human courage, endurance, and aspiration. There can be no doubt that Browning's work marks one of the chief accomplishments in the Victorian Period.

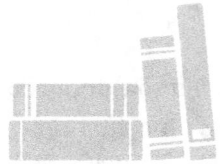

THE VICTORIAN POETS

TEXTUAL ANALYSIS

MATTHEW ARNOLD

INTRODUCTION

Arnold, in a letter to his mother in 1869, wrote an evaluation of his poetry and a prediction of its future popularity which is accurate enough to deserve quoting:

> My poems represent, on the whole, the main movement of mind of the last quarter of a century, and thus they will probably have their day as people become conscious to themselves of what that movement of mind is, and interested in the literary productions which reflect it. It might be fairly urged that I have less poetical sentiment than Tennyson, and less intellectual vigor and abundance than Browning; yet, because I have perhaps more of a fusion of the two than either of them, and have more regularly applied that fusion to the main line

of modern development, I am likely enough to have my turn, as they have had theirs.

Arnold's estimate of his future reputation, which at the time may have sounded like an effort at self-consolation for the fact that he was less popular than Tennyson or Browning, has proven to be true. Long regarded as the inferior in this trio of major Victorian poets, today he enjoys an appreciation which sometimes goes beyond that of Tennyson or Browning. Those critics who would rank his poetry above that of his two contemporaries do so for precisely the reasons that Arnold analyzed. Because he is less extreme than Tennyson in his melancholia and less aggressive than Browning in his enthusiasm for life, he appeals to many modern readers who regard either tendency carried too far as ludicrous. He is often spoken of as the most "modern" of the Victorians in that he sees clearly the dilemma of man living in a mechanized world without the strength of traditional religion to support him and lacking any substitute for spiritual nourishment. But he is less vacillating than Tennyson in his moods of dark withdrawal or wishful optimism and less confident than Browning that man by just believing in himself could win over the forces of evil. His approach to the dilemma is more moderate and thoughtful. He honestly faces the fact that he cannot believe in orthodox Christianity, as he understood it, in the face of scientific discoveries. Ceaselessly he searches for a valid substitute for the union of meaning and values which a belief in religion gives. Unlike Tennyson he does not take refuge in the inner promptings of his heart that there is a God and "faintly trust the larger hope." Nor, like Browning, does he rejoice in the battle of life made even more glorious because more unaided. Rather he explores the resources of man and finds some hope in the power of literature as an effective guide to replace religion. Most of this exploration is carried on in his criticism. There always remains, however, a recognition that man is a weak as well as a noble creature.

Rather than evolving progressively upward, man actually may be losing the battle over the uncivilized forces of nature and society. This is the **theme** he explores in his poetry. This strain of quiet determination to do one's best in what may very well be a losing fight, and in doing so at least preserve the dignity of the term "human being" is characteristic of Arnold's poetry.

While it is clear that Arnold has earned a place for himself as a major Victorian poet and as one who has something to say to the twentieth century, it is not likely that even his ardent admirers can hoist his reputation over that of Tennyson and Browning. Arnold wrote comparatively little poetry, and most of that before 1860. For the last thirty years of his life he devoted himself almost exclusively to prose criticism. Some of his appeal today seems to be won by default. Because he wrote less than Browning or Tennyson he also wrote less bad poetry. And he also had less space in which to reiterate his ideas to the point where they became annoying, as in his contemporaries.

EARLY LIFE AND EDUCATION

Arnold was born in 1822 in Laleham, a village in the Thames valley. Dr. Thomas Arnold, Matthew's father, was appointed headmaster of the famous Rugby school when Matthew was six, and so the young boy was more than assured of growing up in an educated circle. His father was well-known in his own right as a classical scholar and a leader of the liberal or Broad Church movement. Thomas Arnold's influence on his son is readily apparent. Matthew read the classics in the original Greek and Latin and the Bible in Hebrew as a student, and their impact on his ideas is at the core of his poetry and criticism. As a leader of the Evangelical movement, which opposed the High Church tendencies of John Henry Newman and the Oxford Movement,

Arnold Senior was most interested in the Church as a moral and social force. He preached the importance of a high standard of virtue and the necessity of devoting oneself to the improvement of society. Although Matthew Arnold was not able to support his father's religious tenets as an adult, his concern for personal integrity and devotion to the common good were lifelong.

In 1841 Arnold went to Oxford to continue his education, but he earned a reputation as a dandy and gayblade rather than as a scholar. There was nothing superficial about Arnold's refinement, however, and his prose works reveal a light, humorous touch which is quite lacking in his poetry. It almost seems that Arnold's poetry is a disclosure of his inner feelings, while his prose is like the outward behavior he maintained throughout his life, stable but not solemn. In 1844 he managed to earn a degree by some intensive studying and the next year he was elected a fellow of Oriel College, Oxford. He left in 1847 to take the post of private secretary to Lord Lansdowne, who, as Lord President of the Council, was head of the educational undertakings of the government. Unlike Tennyson and Browning, Arnold could not give his full time to writing, which may account in part for his lesser productivity.

1849 FIRST VOLUME OF POETRY

The Strayed Reveller and Other Poems was published in 1849. Its title is significant in that these poems reveal a side of Arnold hitherto unfamiliar to his family and friends, the contemplative. The poem which gives the collection its title is autobiographical in spirit and displays Arnold's already strong command of Greek mythology. The poem is a semi-dramatic piece with three speakers, the Youth, Circe, and Ulysses. The Youth, who is the principal speaker, strays from the festival honoring Bacchus into the palace of Circe, the enchantress. She gives him wine to drink which puts him into a dreamlike state wherein he envisions many wonderful things, including the divine Bacchus, god of the arts. As the poem ends he begs Circe for more of the enchanting potion so that he can experience more quickly and more intensely the fullness of life in order to create poetry out of his experiences. The youth in the poem is actually a Keatsian type figure who feels he must experience all, be a part of all life has to offer and yet not commit himself, in order to have material for his poetry. Arnold's poetic practice was to follow a course much more classical in bent. Although he uses subjective emotional experiences in his poems, he usually objectifies them in a legend or story of some kind and describes them in a manner markedly austere and controlled.

THE FORSAKEN MERMAN

One of the most well-known poems in the 1849 volume is "The Forsaken Merman." Arnold utilized a Danish folktale for this poem, which tells of a merman who is deserted by his mistress and the mother of his children. Tales about forsaken mermaids are common in folklore, but here Arnold uses the less familiar type where the sea inhabitant is male and the human being female. This lyric monologue opens with the merman calling his children to come away from the shore and return to the sea again. But before they leave he asks them to call their mother once more, and perhaps she will return to them. But the mother does not come. She returned to earth when she heard the church bells signalling Easter time:

> 'Twill be Easter time in the world - ah me!
> And I lose my poor soul, Merman! here with thee.
> **(lines 58 - 59)**

The merman told her to go up to the world and say a prayer, expecting that she would come back to the sea cave again. At last the merman despairs of her ever returning, seeing that she is determined to remain on earth despite her "sorrow-clouded eye" and a "heart sorrow-laden" because of the loss of her family.

"The Forsaken Merman" is open to several interpretations, although on the surface it is a simple ballad-like poem which tells a story. The technique of repetition found in **ballads** is effective herein conveying an unearthly, eerie, desolate quality to the poem. Each **stanza** begins with a variation on the opening lines:

Come, dear children, let us away;
Down and away below!

The name of the lady who deserts her lover is Margaret. During the summers of 1848 and 1849 Arnold was apparently very attracted to a French girl named Marguerite. Little is known about the relationship, but it seems that Arnold decided he could not marry her because of their different backgrounds. Perhaps Arnold in this poem is giving expression to the sense of loss he feels over Marguerite, even if he was the one to make the decision to separate. But it is not necessary to confine the poem to a strictly autobiographic interpretation. The poem certainly could be a symbolic expression of the conflict between the world of desire and the world of duty. Margaret is afraid that she will lose her soul if she remains with the merman. Once on earth she is contented in her daily routine and her observance of duty, but she sometimes deeply mourns the loss of her former life. The merman cannot survive on earth so he must return to the sea. Perhaps Arnold is suggesting that sometimes man must foresake what he loves very deeply for the higher calling of moral duty, but he does not cease to regret his loss even in his satisfaction with doing what is right. The separation is a permanent one because the two ways of life can never exist together. Other Victorian poets have expressed similar ideas, including Tennyson, in an age which often saw a very clear dichotomy between pleasure and duty. The turning away of Arnold from poetry to prose criticism in the last thirty years of his life is sometimes interpreted by critics as a decision to turn from the pleasure of imaginative creation to the more austere calling of social reform through **didactic** criticism. Certainly Arnold regarded the transition from youth to maturity as a definite break between freedom and responsibility. In 1851 he wrote to his sister:

The aimless and unsettled, but also open and liberal state of our youth we must perhaps all leave and take refuge in our morality and character; but with most of us it is a melancholy passage.

TO A FRIEND AND SHAKESPEARE

Two other poems which are often anthologized from the 1849 volume are "To a Friend" and "Shakespeare." Both of these poems communicate a sense of sorrow which springs from living in these "bad days." But the poet can find comfort in the great literature of the past. In "To A Friend" he expresses his admiration for the great classical writers Homer, Epictetus, and particularly Sophocles. Arnold was a great upholder of the classical virtues of moderation, balance and control, in thought and style, throughout his life. He opposed, on the whole, the Romantic poet's attitude towards literature as a form of self-expression requiring extreme personal experiences, such as the Youth believes in "The Strayed Reveller." Arnold thought this was an immature attitude and throughout his literary criticism upholds the classical style over the Romantic. He, therefore, especially admires Sophocles, the Greek dramatist (496 - 406 B.C.), because he "saw life steadily and saw it whole" (Line 10). The companion **sonnet** "Shakespeare" pays tribute to the comprehensive knowledge of man Shakespeare possessed. Arnold follows the tradition of placing Shakespeare above any particular style or period. He thinks of him as a native genius lacking formal education but more knowledgeable than any writer before or since in the "pains" the "weakness" and the "griefs" man must endure.

MARRIAGE AND NEW CAREER

Arnold married Lucy Wightman, daughter of a judge, in 1851. The marriage was a happy one. In order to provide for his family Arnold secured a position as an inspector of schools, through Lord Landsdowne. Arnold held the position for thirty-five years, and he was very sincere in his efforts to improve the educational system of England. The work required much traveling throughout the country inspecting local schools, which amply cut down the amount of time Arnold had for writing poetry. The position did give him the opportunity of visiting the Continent several times to investigate the European school system. These trips naturally broadened Arnold's interest in French, Italian and German literature. As far as his literary output is concerned, the only work directly connected with his official duties of any literary merit is *A French Eton* published in 1864.

1852 EMPEDOCLES ON ETNA

One of Arnold's most ambitious works, is the long dramatic poem *Empedocles on Etna*. Empedocles was a Greek philosopher who lived in Sicily in the fifth century B.C. He was supposed to have met his death by jumping into the crater of Mount Etna. Arnold does much the same thing with his treatment of this historical figure as Tennyson did with Ulysses, Arthur, etc; that is, he is concerned with him as a symbol of man as he is in the nineteenth century rather than as an actual person living in a much different time and place. Arnold wrote in the Preface to *Poems*, 1853 that he intended to delineate the feelings of a philosopher living in a time:

> **...when the habits of Greek thought and feeling had begun fast to change, character to dwindle, the influence of the Sophists to prevail. Into the feelings of a man so situated there entered much that we are accustomed to consider as exclusively modern...**

In the poem Empedocles represents the life of reason, and Callicles, the life of the imagination. Empedocles had once been a poet like Callicles, but abandoned his earlier calling in order to devote himself to the rational study of man. In Act One Empedocles describes the world where traditional ethical and religious ideas are no longer valid. He offers Callicles a philosophy of life which is largely stoical: curbing one's desires and submitting oneself to the will of the universe, asking only the will power to endure calamity. But Empedocles himself is unable to achieve the peace of mind which comes from self-dependence and detachment from the world, and in the end he commits suicide. Callicles survives to continue his life of poetic contemplation which feeds his soul with visions of what has been and what could be. Empedocles is destroyed by the relentless logic of abstract thought.

Empedocles on Etna is to some extent an imaginative embodiment of the conflict in Arnold's mind over whether to dedicate his life to poetry or the public service. It also reflects Arnold's own attraction to the Stoical philosophy of self-denial at the same time that he is repelled by the equilibrium which is achieved at the cost of castigating the senses and emotions.

1853 POEMS

Arnold published an important collection of poems in 1853 to which he added a Preface, which was his first important piece of literary criticism. The volume itself contains some of Arnold's most famous works. One group of six love poems is entitled Switzerland and centers about the poet's love for a girl named Marguerite. As in "The Forsaken Merman" they tell of a love between two individuals which is broken because of moral duty which demands they separate. Arnold uses the image of an ocean which separates two continents to describe effectively the division between the lovers. Once they were united, "parts of a single continent." But now they are forever divided, just as the single land mass of the world long ago became separated by the ocean. Arnold's quiet control over a line, which suggests the power of the emotion and yet distances it, is evident in the following:

> A God, a God their severance ruled!
> And bade betwixt their shores to be
> The unplumbed, salt, estranging sea.

THE BURIED LIFE

This is another poem in the 1853 volume in which Arnold uses the **imagery** of water, this time of a buried stream which flows indiscernibly underground and is only seen at isolated intervals. The buried stream is a symbol of the hidden life of man, his true self which he keeps hidden for the most part under a veneer of acquired social behavior. Man does not have the courage to face himself as he really is, to pursue the "nameless feelings" which course through his breast. These feelings remain suppressed as he avoids facing his true identity and conforms to the mores of his associates. But if he is very fortunate and is able to share a rare moment with his beloved where they actually communicate, the mask of appearance will be torn aside and for once he will come to know himself. At this time he will become aware of "the buried life," the mystery of his existence and individuality, and he will possess a peace of mind he has never felt before.

"The Buried Life" has a certain modern tone about it. The poets and prose writers of the twentieth century are very preoccupied with the difference between appearance and reality. Influenced by Freudian psychology they are aware that man submerges much of his true personality under a mask of socially approved behavior. Arnold does not use the vocabulary of modern psychology, but he describes the sublimation of man's inner feelings in order to conform to society's standards:

> **There rises an unspeakable desire**
> **After the knowledge of our buried life;**
> **A thirst to spend our fire and restless force**
> **In tracking out our true, original course. (lines 47-50)**

Arnold finds hope in the communion which love brings, a communion which some modern writers doubt is possible in the fragmented world of the twentieth century:

> **And there arrives a lull in the hot race**
> **Wherein he doth forever chase**

> That flying and elusive shadow, rest.
> An air of coolness plays upon his face,
> And an unwonted calm pervades his breast.

PHILOMELA

Arnold turns again to Greek legend in his lyric poem "Philomela." He uses the version of the tale in which Philomela is married to the king of Trace. Her husband rapes Philomela's sister Procne and then cuts out her tongue to prevent her from revealing the secret. Procne, however, weaves the story of her outrage into a tapestry, and Philomela learns the truth and avenges the deed. She is then transformed into a nightingale. Arnold tells the story as a symbol of the universal and timeless plight of mankind which is to suffer and endure. The poem is effective in that the poet uses the nightingale as an eternal victim of man's inhumanity to man, rather than bemoaning the particular state of its Victorian counterpart. He does not directly describe the experience of Philomela, but suggests it and relies on his reader's knowledge of the legend. The poems opens with the poet listening to the sound of a nightingale and then deliberately addressing it as a "wanderer from a Grecian shore" that after many years still nourishes "That wild, unquenched, deep-sunken, old-world pain." The poet is perfectly aware, of course, that this is not the same nightingale, but he wants to emphasize that in every land, in every age, sorrow and suffering are the fate of mankind:

> How thick the burst come crowding through the leaves!
> Again - thou hearest?
> Eternal passion!
> Eternal pain!

THE SCHOLAR GYPSY

One of the important poems in the 1853 volume is "The Scholar Gypsy." It tells of a seventeenth-century Oxford student who left the University to join a band of gypies in their travels. Arnold's source for the poem was Joseph Glanvill's *Vanity of Dogmatizing* (1661) which reports the story as actual fact. At the outset of the poem the poet addresses a shepherd who has been helping him search for traces of the scholar gypsy and bids him return to his duties of taking care of the sheep. The poet says he will wait until evening to renew his quest with the help of the shepherd. Glanvill's book is lying on the grass, and the poet picks it up to reread the story of the Oxford scholar who was too poor to make his way in the world and too proud to beg for preferment. One day he forsook his friends to join a band of traveling gypsies, and he never returned to Oxford. Once some of his old friends met him and upon inquiry the wandering scholar told them that the gypsies had secret knowledge of men's minds and that he was intent on learning their art so that he could tell the world. Arnold imagines that the scholar still lives, and dressed in his antique clothes has been seen by various country people at different times of the year. Arousing himself from his reverie the poet realizes that he has been dreaming and that the scholar has been dead two hundred years. But he then grasps the reason why rumors continue to persist, even in the nineteenth century, that the scholar gypsy lives. The spirit of the scholar is immortal and what he represents to man is timeless. He did not waste his life pursuing vain material gain, but had the courage to leave the world and pursue with singleness of purpose the hidden meaning of life, to await the "spark from heaven:"

> **For early didst thou leave the world, with powers**
> **Fresh, undiverted to the world without,**
> **Firm to their mark, not spent on other things,**

> Free from the sick fatigue, the languid doubt,
> Which much to have tried, in much been baffled, brings
> O life unlike to ours!

Modern man also awaits "the spark from heaven," but it never comes because, unlike the scholar, he lives in a world which distracts him from his true purpose:

> O born in days when wits were fresh and clear,
> And life ran gaily as the sparkling Thames;
> Before this strange disease of modern life,
> With its sick hurry, its divided aims,
> Its heads o'ertaxed, it palsied hearts, was rife -
> Fly hence, our contact fear!

The poem concludes with a **simile** which is somewhat obscure, but is meant to suggest a parallel to the scholar's choice of gypsy life. Arnold urges the perennial youth to flee contact with modern life lest he lose his purpose and so grow old and die. He bids him to escape just as long ago in classical times the Tyrian trader fled from his ancient home in the Aegean islands, when he saw its peace being intruded upon by noisy Greek merchants. The Tyrian trader fled to the Spanish peninsula where he made his home with the Iberian gypsies. This comparison is rather confusing, since the Tyrian trader is a merchant with a definite commercial purpose in mind. On the other hand, Arnold is rather vague about the aim of the scholar gypsy, other than that he flees civilization to find his true purpose in nature.

The similarities between "The Buried Life" and "The Scholar Gypsy" are apparent. Both urge the abandonment of society and its preordained way of life in order to seek deeper knowledge of oneself. Like Tennyson's "Ulysses," the search seems to be more important than the goal. Arnold is rather indefinite bout what it is that is "buried," what one is to seek. But perhaps he is purposely vague in order to emphasize that each individual must find out for himself the purposes which will give life meaning and pursue it helped by the resources for contemplation to be found in nature. Both poems use the **imagery** of a quietly flowing river whose source and destination must be sought out to suggest the course of man's life, although this latter image is only suggested in "The Scholar Gypsy." The latter poem is indebted to Arnold's knowledge and love of pastoral poetry, particularly the idylls of Theocritus. He describes the countryside surrounding Oxford with details which remind us of Wordswoth: the "Dark bluebells drenched with dews of summer eves," the children who range the hills, the housewife who mends at her open door, but his language is more stylized following the formal pastoral tradition.

SOHRAB AND RUSTUM

The 1853 volume contained one of Arnold's most popular works, *Sohrab and Rustum*. Its ultimate source is an **epic** poem on Persian history, the Shah-Nama, written by Firdausi. Arnold was fascinated with the possibilities for tragic poetry offered by the story of a father, Sohrab, who kills his son, Rustum, in battle, unaware of his son's identity. Sohrab was the offspring of an early love affair of Rustum. Rustum had left the mother and gained fame as a great soldier in the Persian army. Fearful that she might lose her son, Sohrab's mother wrote to Rustum that the child was a daughter. When the son was grown, he enlisted under Afrasiab, King of the Tartars, and was a great warrior against the Persians. Rustum, as a great Persian soldier, resolved to fight Sohrab and defeat him. Fighting and finally mortally wounds him. When Sohrab is dying, he warns under a feigned name, as was the custom, the father meets his son Rustum to beware of the vengeance of his father when he discovers the deed. At this point both father and son learn the truth about each other. But it is too late, and the grieving father is left to bury his son.

This poem, written in **blank verse**, was one of Arnold's personal favorites. He felt the subject was an excellent one because it could be expressed in terms of dramatic **irony** and action. Unlike *Empedocles on Etna*, which Arnold refused to reprint in the 1853 volume, he felt that the suffering of the **protagonist** found vent in action, rather than venting itself in prolonged mental distress "unrelieved by incident, hope, or resistance" (Preface). "Where everything is to be endured and nothing done" (as in the case of *Empedocles on Etna*) "the description of such distress can become morbid and monotonous." Arnold felt that he had succeeded in *Sohrab and Rustum* in describing a situation that was truly tragic, rather than just painful. The father and son become victims of a fate over which they have no control, and which, ironically, they helped to bring about. More than just being an exciting poem appealing to the fundamental human emotions of fear and grief, Arnold felt that *Sohrab and Rustum* had, to some extent, the qualities he demanded of great literature. He wrote to his poet friend Arthur Clough:

> **I am glad you like the Gypsy Scholar, but what does it do for you? Homer animates - Shakespeare animates - in its poor way I think Sohrab and Rustum animates - the Gypsy Scholar at best awakens a pleasing melancholy. But this is not what we want. 'The complaining millions of men Darken in labour and pain' - what they want is something to animate and ennoble them.**

Arnold was to reiterate this sentiment in much of his literary criticism. It is the foundation of his attitude towards the value of literature. He felt that it was not enough for a writer to be entertaining or informative. He must uplift the reader in a positive way, making him conscious of the grandeur of the human spirit and giving him hope to continue striving. In this sense literature could be a substitute for formal religion by providing man with ideals to live by founded in human experience rather than formal theology.

THYRSIS

By the middle of the 1850's Arnold's poetic output was beginning to decline steadily. Partly this was due to the heavy pressure of work that kept him constantly traveling as an inspector of schools. Partly it seems to have been due to Arnold's own dissatisfaction with his poetry. In the 1853 Preface he had stated that great poetry should be objective; that is, its subject matter should lend itself to **epic** or dramatic treatment rather than lyrical. But it was obvious to Arnold that despite his excursions into **epic** (*Sohrab and Rustum*) or dramatic (*Merope, Tristram and Iseult*) poetry, his real talent lay precisely in the realm of poetry he now repudiated. His best efforts turned out to be personal lamentations expressing the melancholy, the ennui, the loneliness, and the quiet despair of modern life. Although distanced by the use of myth or symbol, they still were essentially lyrics in the elegiac mood.

One of the finest of Arnold's poems in the second category is his elegy commemorating the death of Arthur Hugh Clough, "Thyrsis." The poem was published in 1866, five years after the death of Clough in Florence, Italy. Arnold calls the **elegy** a "monody," which is a lament in which a single mourner expresses his grief. The **elegy** draws upon the Greek and Latin pastoral tradition and is similar, in its use of shepherds against a rustic background to portray the chief figures, to Milton's and Shelley's pastoral elegies, "Lycidas," and "Adonais." Arnold modelled the **diction** on the formal but graceful style of Theocritus, (Third century, B.C.).

The scene of the **elegy** is the university town of Oxford and its environs, where Arnold and Clough went to college. It is the same setting as that of "The Scholar Gypsy," and this figure functions symbolically in the poem. In the opening lines the poet remarks on the mutability that time brings to all that "man makes or fills." The villages of North Hinksley and South Hinksley have changed since the author was there as a student with Clough, which is now many years ago. The poet recalls the familiar scenes of his university days, the path leading into the high wood, the hill where they watched the flaming sunset, the Thames river. Now he no longer can find his way effortlessly among the fields. Even the elm tree which he and Clough thought of as symbolic of the eternal spirit of the gypsy scholar is gone. Arnold recalls the happy times of the past when he and Clough wandered through the fields, making friends with the country folk, and beginning their first poetic efforts, "Here, too, our shepherd pipes we first assayed." But that time was all too brief. Arnold had to go into the world to make his living, and Clough left the University rather than subscribe to the Anglican Church, at that time a requirement to lecture there. Clough's subsequent poetry was concerned with the political and religious controversy of the day. He lost the peace he knew at Oxford and never lived to regain it:

He went; his piping took a troubled sound
Of storms that rage outside our happy ground;
He could not wait their passing, he is dead.
(lines 49-51)

Arnold compares Clough's departure to that of the Cuckoo who leaves after the first burst of spring blossoming is over and, too quickly despairing, never sees the bloom of midsummer. So too Thyrsis has left, not just Oxford but life. Too quickly despairing over the lost spring of his youth, he will never know the productivity of middle age. The stanza describing the lovely flowers of midsummer is drawn from the pastoral elegiac tradition (Cf. "Lycidas"). Besides lending a formal beauty to the lament, the description of the flowers, symbols of fragile but fleeting loveliness, is appropriate to the elegiac **theme** . The flowers suggest the inevitability of death destroying beauty, but they also suggest rebirth as the seasons repeat their cycle.

But Arnold despairs of Thyrsis' return, "For Time, not Corydon, hath conquered thee!" During their stay at Oxford Arnold and Clough would compete with each other to write the best poetry, but now Arnold (Corydon) laments that he is not a better poet. He wishes he could compose a lament as powerful as those of the ancient past, such as the Greek poet Moschus wrote for his fellow shepherd Bion, which was powerful enough to bring the dead back to life. Yet Corydon continues his quest for the elm tree which had a special meaning for the two friends, for grief must have its hour even if the words are in vain.

The tree which Corydon is searching for gradually takes on its symbolic function. Its association in the minds of the two friends with the story of the scholar gypsy (see Arnold's poem of this title) who spent his life searching for hidden truth, inner meaning, lends the tree the same quality of immortality possessed by the scholar.

As Corydon searches for the tree the night descends, and he finds it more and more difficult to move on. Arnold is clearly describing more than the coming of night, which makes it more difficult to find one's way along the realistic countryside. He is also suggesting the coming of his own old age, whose approach is almost welcome. For death will bring an end to what seems like vain "earthly turmoil" after the bright hope of youth is gone.

But the coming of sunset emblazons the steep mountain path, and at last Arnold sees the tree which he had thought was gone. In the midst of his joy, however, he realizes that Thyrsis is not there to share his victory. Clough is buried in Florence and listens to a much different music than that provided by English fields. But the Gypsy Scholar lives to wander the countryside to search for a "fugitive and gracious light," that does not come with houses, gold, honor, or any of the things for which men strive. At last Arnold finds consolation in the symbol of the tree. For just as Arnold and Clough sought the tree, and Arnold continues to search for it, so they strove to find the truth. Thyrsis shares in the immortality of the seventeenth century gypsy scholar because he too left the university on a spiritual quest for truth. The only promise of immortality which Arnold can offer is that which comes from devoting one's life to searching for spiritual meaning and having the example of one's quest live on to inspire others. So Arnold is consoled by the meaning of Clough's life, which says to him:

> **Why faintest thou? I wandered till I died.**
> **Roam on! The light we sought is shining still.**
> **Dost thou ask proof? Our tree yet crowns the hill,**
> **Our Scholar travels yet the loved hillside.**
> **(lines 237-240)**

DOVER BEACH

The last volume of Arnold's poems appeared in 1867, the year he finished his ten year tenure as Professor of Poetry at Oxford.

After the publication of *New Poems* Arnold devoted himself almost exclusively to literary and social criticism. This last book contains the most popular of Arnold's poems for the twentieth-century reader, "Dover Beach." This lyric has as its **theme** the sense of despair which accompanies the loss of faith which is so characteristic of Arnold's poetry in general, and can also be often seen in Tennyson. But the mood is so modulated, helped by the austere **diction** and **imagery**, that it seems, more/than/ any other lyric of the age, to sum up the Victorian temper as felt by men of learning and sensitivity.

The poet stands at the window watching the scene below. It is a lovely, calm night. The waves quietly beat against the cliffs of Dover, and across the straights the glimmering lights of the French coast can be seen. There is one sound, however, that destroys the tranquility of the scene for the poet. It is the grating sound of the pebbles on the beach, as they are flung onto the shore, drawn back by the waves, and flung on the beach again in a never ending cycle. To the poet this grating roar symbolizes the suffering which has always been part of man's landscape:

> **Begin, and Cease, and then again begin,**
> **With tremulous cadence slow, and bring**
> **The eternal note of sadness in.**

The poet recalls that the great Greek dramatic poet Sophocles heard this same sound long ago on the Aegean sea (Cf. Antigone, lines 583 ff.), and the sound suggested the "turbid ebb and flow/ Of human misery" to him then just as it now suggests it to Arnold. But the ebbing of the tide brings to mind something more to Arnold today. It reminds him that "The Sea of Faith," specifically Christianity but more generally any belief in a supreme Being or Beings, is also retreating after having one encircled the earth.

In this modern world where the only constancy is suffering, with no succor to be found in religion, the only hope is love. In the last stanza the poet tells his loved one that they must be true to one another, for the world which looks so beautiful before them knows no joy, nor love, nor peace:

> And we are here as on a darkling plain
> Swept with confused alarms of struggle and flight
> Where ignorant armies clash by night.

This last **metaphor** is powerful. Arnold pictures modern life as a battlefield where night is approaching, and man does not know whether he should continue the fight to survive or flee from the world. The poetry of Arnold, Tennyson and Browning, of course, among other writers, urged these different courses to the reader. The last line is the most frightening of all. Man is not even a knowing agent in this battle, but rather part of a huge multitude whose destinies are not controlled by themselves.

CONCLUSION

After the publication of the 1867 *New Poems* Arnold turned his talent exclusively to the writing of literary and social criticism. Although a consideration of his critical prose is not within the realm of this study, it is important to know that Arnold is as much studied today for his critical ideas as for his poetry. Arnold is really the forerunner of the critic-poets of the twentieth century, such as T.S. Eliot, who have elevated English literary criticism from a minor **genre** peripheral to literature to a major area of creative endeavor. Although some of Arnold's critical premises would seem very wrong-headed and outdated to his successors, certain of his ideas are still well received. Arnold's classicism, his emphasis on objectivity in literature, his insistence on the poem being considered as a unity, and even his urbane, slightly ironic prose style are characteristic of Eliot. And the extension of Arnold's criticism into the areas of culture, society and religion also anticipates Eliot, although their attitudes in these areas are vastly different.

ESSAYS IN CRITICISM

Essays in Criticism (First Series, 1865) formalizes the ideas adumbrated in the Preface to the 1853 *Poems*, which have been referred to in this chapter. *Culture and Anarchy* (1869) is Arnold's most famous work of social criticism. It is tempting to apply the ideas and standards of Arnold's criticism to his poetry. Such a procedure can have only limited value. To note T.S. Eliot once again, where a similar approach can be made, he remarks that "in one's prose reflections one may be legitimately occupied with ideals, whereas in the writing of verse, one can deal only with actuality." This is certainly true of Arnold. As a poet he was concerned with the despair on the individual poisoned with "this strange disease of modern life." As a critic, Arnold was concerned with finding a cure for this disease.

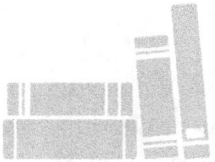

THE VICTORIAN POETS

TEXTUAL ANALYSIS

DANTE GABRIEL ROSSETTI

....

INTRODUCTION

The Victorian scene presented a considerable number of problems and intellectual uncertainties upon which the poet might draw for subject matter. The poetry of Tennyson, Browning, and Arnold, each to varying degrees, reflects the temper, the skepticism, the search for faith of their age. Yet the work of the Pre-Raphaelite Brotherhood (see introductory chapter) reflects a different attitude, one that anticipates the later aesthetic movement of such men as Oscar Wilde and Walter Pater. The poetry of Dante Gabriel Rossetti takes as its starting point a view that art must be concerned exclusively with the portrayal of the beautiful, and not with useful or **didactic** intentions. Rossetti has been referred to as "the poet-painter" and his work reveals a rich pictorial as well as a vital poetic faculty. He was, of course, a painter of considerable power, and his poetry at all times reflects the pictorial artist's approach to subject. The Pre-Raphaelite Brotherhood was a group of young artists and men of letters whose principal object was to reform English painting by rejecting the established academic style. They sought a return to the rich simplicity of pre-Renaissance art. Although the Brotherhood did not cohere for many years, Rossetti himself always closely adhered to his view that: "Color and meter, these are the true patents of nobility in painting and poetry, taking precedence of all intellectual claims."

LIFE

Dante Gabriel Rossetti was born in London in 1828, the son of an exiled Italian patriot. His father's political activities in Italy had forced him to flee to England to escape Austrian tyranny. The Rossetti household was one wherein liberal politics and other controversial subjects were hotly debated, but the son never aspired to his father's political interests. The Rossetti home was also a center of rich cultural activity, and the father was an intense student of the great Italian poet Dante, author of *The Divine Comedy*. Indeed Dante became a kind of familiar spirit in the Rossetti home, and the son was to continue his father's enthusiasm.

INFLUENCE OF DANTE AND KEATS

Rossetti showed promise as a boy and his early interest was art. The beauty of colors and particularly the beauty of women's faces and figures interested him and provided a world that was detached from the Victorian scene. His view of art and life was greatly influenced by his early and close reading of the letters and poetry of John Keats, the Romantic poet. A greater influence was the work of Dante. As a boy Rossetti read *The Divine Comedy* and was especially attracted to the kind of mysticism which he found there. Dante's *Vita Nuova* also influenced him. Rossetti's personal mysticism responded to Dante's conception of the fulfillment of human love and beauty in the divine, a view obviously important in the figure of Beatrice in the Paradiso section of *The Divine Comedy*. Rossetti also early delighted in the medieval world of romance and chivalry which he discovered in the works of Keats, Scott, and the fifteenth century romance writer Malory. Thus this imaginative world of medieval times, rich in color, pageantry, and ideals of love, provided Rossetti with an escape from what he considered the drabness of his own age. In art he sought a return to the times of Giotto (1276?-1337?) and Leonardo da Vinci (1452-1519), and of certain early Flemish and German painters, whom he believed possessed an emotional sincerity and decorative charm worthy of emulation. The Pre-Raphaelite Brotherhood of 1848 is tangible evidence of the seriousness with which Rossetti sought to embody his aesthetic views in art. Rossetti's brother, William, said that the basis of the new attempt was to be "serious and elevated invention of subject, along with earnest scrutiny of visible facts, and an earnest endeavour to present them veraciously and exactly."

THE BLESSED DAMOZEL

The word "damozel" in the title of this poem is an early form of damsel. Rossetti attributed the origin of "The Blessed Damozel" to his reading of Edgar Allan Poe's Raven, a poem which he admired. Rossetti commented as follows: "I saw that Poe had done the utmost it was possible to do with the grief of the lover on earth, and so I determined to reverse the conditions, and give utterance to the yearning of the loved one in heaven." "The Blessed Damozel" is the best of the poems contributed by Rossetti to *The Germ*, a magazine that was started in 1850 by the Pre-Raphaelite group to spread their literary ideas. The magazine did not have a long life. The speaker in the poem is the lover who imagines that he sees the blessed damozel leaning out from heaven and looking upon him below. He further imagines that the falling autumn leaves caressing his face are her hair. The poem is written in six line **stanzas** of alternating iambic **tetrameter** and **trimeter**. It is now ten years since the damozel left earth, and the lover communicates his dream in opulent and sensuous terms:

> **The blessed damozel leaned out**
> **From the gold bar of heaven;**
> **Her eyes were deeper than the depth**
> **Of waters stilled at even;**
> **She had three lilies in her hand,**
> **And the stars in her hair were seven.**

One should note the lushness and the sensuous appeal of the imagery apparent in the opening **stanza** quoted above and throughout the entire poem. Such **imagery** testifies to the powerful pictorial imagination of Rossetti. In the second **stanza** the damozel's robe is portrayed and we learn that it is adorned with a "white rose of Mary's gift." The rose is here used as a symbol of virginity. The question of time is presented in that the lover indicates that the damozel has been dead for ten years, and yet she feels she has been one of God's choristers but a day. He sees newly met lovers around her and souls of the blessed winging their way to heaven "like thin flames." She speaks to him of the time to come when he will join her in heaven and of their prayers to that purpose. She says that Mary will bring them "hand in hand" to Him, and:

> **"There will I ask of Christ the Lord**
> **Thus much for him and me-**

> Only to live as once on earth
> With Love - only to be,
> As then awhile, forever now,
> Together, I and he."

The damozel smiles at this thought, casts her arms along the golden barriers of heaven, and "laid her face between her hands,/ And wept. (I heard her tears.)" The conclusion indicates that their human love will only find completion when they are joined in heaven- the contrast of the damozel's smile and her tears is important.

"The Blessed Damozel" obviously embodies the ideals of the Pre-Raphaelite group, and in many ways the poem is one of the most noteworthy examples of their beliefs. The subject is a very elevated one because the concern is with the fulfillment of human love in a spiritual sense. Yet the reader should notice that the inhabitants of heaven are presented in very vivid and naturalistic description, and further, the emphasis upon color in the poem (e. g., gold, white) lends a sense of lushness. The heaven of the poem is certainly rich with radiant physical bodies. Despite the obvious influence of Dante's Beatrice upon "The Blessed Damozel," the poem differs in that its main appeal is a sensuous one rather than a magnificent presentation of a thoroughly intellectual and spiritual conception of love. What is striking about Rossetti's poem is what has been called his "plastic effect," his ability to approximate closely poetry and painting.

MY SISTER'S SLEEP

This poem concerns the watch for the coming of Christmas Day, but the speaker's sister dies when the clock strikes twelve. The speaker and his mother then kneel and pray: "'Christ's blessing on the newly born!'" This poem indicates Rossetti's treatment of a modern scene, but the close attention to physical detail and description of the interior of the house reveal his characteristic pictorial style. The four line stanza rhyming abba and in iambic **tetrameter** that we find in this poem was also used by Tennyson in "In Memoriam". "Jenny" by Rossetti reveals the influence of Browning's **dramatic monologue** form although here again the pictorial aspect is dominant.

SISTER HELEN

This poem takes a medieval subject and is in dialogue form between Helen and her little brother. At the end of each exchange between Helen and her brother there appears a short prayer which begins "O Mother, Mary Mother..." The poem opens:

> **"Why did you melt your waxen man, Sister Helen?**
> **Today is the third since you began."**
> **"The time was long, yet the time ran, Little brother."**
> **(O Mother, Mary Mother,**
> **Three days today, between Hell and Heaven!)**

The reference to the waxen man of the opening line is to the superstition that melting a waxen image of a person will bring about that person's suffering and death. The brother asks Helen if he may play outside, but before he goes the tread of horses is heard. Three horsemen from "Boyne Bar" appear; one of the riders is Keith of Eastholm who cries "Halloo." Keith announces the news that "Keith of Ewern's like to die." The brother tells the news to Helen, but her reply is "And he and thou, and I,/ Little brother." Three days ago on his marriage morning Keith of Ewern became ill, and now "he prays in torment to be dead."

Helen says that if he prays his request will be granted and he will die. But on this day Keith of Ewern has cried for Helen to take her curse away. Helen says: "My prayer was heard - he need but pray." All of Helen's answers point only to the fact that she will not help. Her heart once melted for Keith of Ewern, but now things have taken a different course. Keith of Westholm returns to say that Keith of Ewern wishes to see Helen before he dies, and he sends Helen "a ring and a broken coin." Thus we learn that Helen and Keith had pledged their troth by breaking the coin with each one keeping half. Keith of Keith, father of the dying Ewern, comes to ask Helen's pardon for his son, but she answers: "Fire shall forgive me as I forgive." Here Helen means that the fire of Hell will burn me just as I burn this waxen image; in no case will there be forgiveness. A further aspect of Helen's curse is that Ewern's soul shall never find peace but remain between heaven and hell. The lady of Ewern, the bride of but three days, comes but is so sorely grieved that she cannot speak. Yet she clasps her hands to heaven and makes lament- a sorrow which Helen terms "her soul's blithe tune." The death bell is heard and the three steeds ride off. It is the signal of Ewern's death. The wax drops from the image, and a "white thing," the soul of Ewern appears in the doorway:

> "Ah! what white thing at the door has crossed, Sister Helen?
> "Ah! what is this that sighs in the frost?"
> "A soul that's lost as mine is lost, Little brother!"
> (O Mother, Mary Mother,
> Lost, lost, all lost, between Hell and Heaven!)

COMMENT ON SISTER HELEN

This narrative is indicative of Rossetti's interest in medieval subjects. As indicated before, Rossetti had a particular affection for color and beauty, and also for romance (Here meaning a tale of adventure in the medieval sense and one based on the code of chivalry. Love was often an important element). "Sister Helen" is one of his best poems revealing these interests. In this poem we get a magical element which is instrumental in effecting the revenge for unrequited love. Helen is demoniacal in her thirst for revenge upon Ewern. The starkness of the scene and of the presentation helps to create the mood of grimness. The exchange of dialogue and the **refrain** which indicates the tossing emotions of Helen are both handled well. Pictorial detail is lacking in this poem; instead there is a concentration on effective narrative, one illustrating in quite vivid terms the jealousy, cruelty, and final despair of Helen.

ELIZABETH SIDDAL

Rossetti was a great lover of physical beauty and in the face of one of his models, Elizabeth Siddal, he believed that he had found the beauty of Dante's Beatrice. Indeed he used Elizabeth as model for his portrait of Beatrice. He fell in love with her in 1850 and married her in 1860. During this period Rossetti translated Dante's *Vita Nuova* and some of his sonnets. In 1861 he published *The Early Italian Poets*, translations of poems by Dante's predecessors and contemporaries, which he later reissued in 1874 under the title Dante and His Circle. Elizabeth Siddal committed suicide in 1862, and this was a great blow to Rossetti, one which was to torment him for the rest of his life. In 1862 Rossetti buried his manuscripts in Elizabeth's coffin. He may well have felt that by this histrionic act he could atone to her for the years of sadness which he felt he had caused her. At the beginning of their relationship Rossetti had viewed Elizabeth under the influence of Dante's mystic ideas of love. However both soon learned that their actuality was in sharp contrast to the ideal of Beatrice and Dante. This realization of the chasm between his ideal of love and its actuality may in part account for the tone of desolation in many of the **sonnets** in *The House of Life*, a sequence which he was writing during these years.

JANE MORRIS

Jane Morris was the wife of Victorian poet William Morris, who was a good friend of Rossetti's. Rossetti fell in love with her and she again became for him a symbol of ideal love. Thus in *The House of Life* there are **sonnets** which express hope in the future, but there is also vain regret for circumstances made Jane Morris simply what might have been for Rossetti.

THE HOUSE OF LIFE

Many poets, such as Sidney, Shakespeare, and Donne, have turned to the **sonnet** form. In the Victorian period Elizabeth Barrett Browning as well as Rossetti wrote **sonnet** sequences. Rossetti's sequence *The House of Life* takes its title from astrology where the heavens are divided into houses and where the chief house is the House of Life. The **sonnets** then are intended to be a comment on life, and they are actually concerned with three major subjects: life, love and death.

The opening **sonnet** is titled "The Sonnet" and in fourteen lines (the traditional length of a **sonnet**) it speaks of what a sonnet should be: "a moment's monument." Throughout the sequence Rossetti employs an adaptation of the five rhymed Italian **sonnet**, which is divided into an octave (eight lines) and a sestet (six lines). The sestet of the opening **sonnet** compares the **sonnet** to a coin whose face reveals the soul and "its converse, to what Power 'tis due." The sestet concludes with the three subjects (life, love and death) mentioned as possible subjects of the sonnet.

SONNETS

Sonnet 4 titled "Lovesight" finds the speaker asking his beloved when he sees her most. He asks if it is in the light or in the dusk hours when his soul sees her soul as his own. The sestet poses the problem that if he should see her no more, then should sound "The wind of Death's imperishable wing." **Sonnet** 19 is titled "Silent Noon" and the speaker is alone with his loved one in a field of grass. The silence of the scene and the beauty of nature are richly pictured. The moment is one sent them from above:

> **So this winged hour is dropped to us from above.**
> **Oh! clasp we to our hearts, for deathless dower,**
> **This close-companioned inarticulate hour**
> **When twofold silence was the song of love.**

Sonnets 97 "A Superscription" and 101 "The One Hope" are both concerned with Jane Morris. The sequence of one hundred and one **sonnets** does not present a consecutive narrative and it is not intended to convey a chronology of psychological moods. The **sonnets** are, in general, quite abstract and are filled with elaborate personification and symbolic imagery.

ROSSETTI'S DEATH

In 1869 Rossetti recovered the manuscripts which were buried with his wife. His eyesight was failing at this time, and he wished to publish them. In 1870 he published *Poems*, a collection of his own work. Robert Buchanan, a Victorian writer, published a review of this volume in the *Contemporary Review*. This review was titled "The Fleshly School of Poetry - Mr. D. G. Rossetti." Buchanan attacked what he felt were the sensualist attitudes in Rossetti's poetry and particularly singled out *The House of Life* as a work containing what he believed were offensive ideas. The sharpness of the attack took its toll on Rossetti who at this time was suffering mental affliction. Rossetti suffered a breakdown and was a different man until his death in 1882.

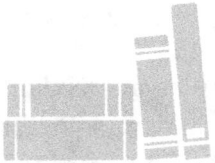

THE VICTORIAN POETS

TEXTUAL ANALYSIS

WILLIAM MORRIS

....

INTRODUCTION AND LIFE

William Morris was born in 1834 at Woodford in Essex, and from his earliest years developed a passionate interest in things medieval. This was stimulated by his early reading of the novels of Sir Walter Scott and by his visits to old cathedrals where he was fascinated by Gothic architecture. He attended boarding school at Marlborough and became an Anglo-Catholic before he entered Oxford in 1853. While at Oxford, Morris read voraciously in the medieval period and prepared to enter the ministry. However, his real interest in Anglo-Catholicism was in its ritual rather than in its theology. He soon gave up this idea to enter the ministry and instead pursued a life devoted to art. Reading influences many men, and in the case of Morris his reading of Malory's *Morte d'Arthur*, of the Romantic poets Keats and Shelley, and of Chaucer, Browning and the early Tennyson, was to leave a lasting effect. John Ruskin, the Victorian critic and essayist, was another very important influence upon Morris.

Ruskin's *Modern Painters*, *The Stones of Venice*, and Thomas Carlyle's *Past and Present* greatly influenced and helped foster Morris's enthusiasm for the medieval.

MORRIS AND ROSSETTI

When Morris gave up his idea of entering the ministry, he decided to become an architect. While studying architecture, he met Rossetti in 1856 and became a disciple of the Pre-Raphaelite Brotherhood. Rossetti's influence led Morris into poetry and painting, and in 1858 Morris published *The Defense of Guenevere and Other Poems*. This publication indicated that there was something new afoot in Victorian poetry. There is some obscurity in this lengthy series of tales on the Arthurian story, but this is largely attributable to the prosodic techniques employed by Morris in trying to break with the patterns established by Tennyson. The conception of the Middle Ages that one finds here is of an age that was barbarous and rough and not at all tinged with Victorian sentiment. This volume could well be the finest of Pre-Raphaelite verse.

THE HAYSTACK IN THE FLOODS

The time of this narrative poem is 1356, just after the English victory over the French at Poitiers. Sir Robert de Marny, an English knight, is riding hard for Gascony which was in English hands, and he is accompanied by his mistress, Jehane. The poem is written in iambic **tetrameter**. Jehane suffers from the cruel weather on the ride and her suffering is compounded when they see Godmar in their path. Robert is determined to go on despite the fears that Jehave voices. He cries "St. George," but there is no answer from his men. Robert is bound and taken prisoner by Godmar who demands that Jehane become his paramour in exchange for the life of Robert de Marny. Jehane is a woman of shady reputation and she is afraid to return to Paris, but she refuses to yield to Godmar. Robert is slain by Godmar, who reminds Jehane that she must make her way back to the Chatelet, a prison in Paris, Jehane concludes the narrative:

> **She shook her head and gazed awhile**
> **At her cold hands with a rueful smile,**
> **As though this thing had made her mad.**
>
> **This was the parting that they had**
> **Beside the haystack in the floods.**

THE EVE OF CRECY

The speaker in this poem is Sir Lambert du Bois, a French knight, who finds himself in poor circumstances. He is dreaming of the wealth and the glory that will accrue to him in the battle of the next day which is the Battle of Crecy (1346). Lambert feels that he will then be able to marry Margaret. The pathos and the **irony** of Lambert's situation lie in the fact that the French were to be defeated on the following day.

THE EARTHLY PARADISE (1868-1870)

This lengthy composition of forty-two thousand lines was published in four volumes in two installments, 1868 and 1870. A group of Germanic, Celtic, and Norse people sail westward to escape the Black Plague and come to an island inhabited by descendants of the ancient Greeks. The Greek descendants have been cut off from the rest of the world and have maintained their culture intact. This situation provided

Morris with a "frame" within which he could contrast the culture of ancient times with the rough, barbarous medieval peoples. The two groups exchange stories and the tellers of the tales are old men looking back upon the glories of their lost youth. In all there are twenty-four stories, two for each month of the year, and the stories are linked together by descriptive interludes. In general the narrative is tedious and there is little individuation of character. The main effect created is that one is looking at a gorgeous tapestry which reveals characters frozen in a moment of time. Yet there is also a sense of vigor, and also a sense of the importance of love and youth. The prefatory poem to *The Earthly Paradise* which is titled "An Apology" finds Morris referring to himself as "The idle singer of an empty day," and the fourth **stanza** indicates the anti-didactic element in Morris:

> **Dreamer of dreams, born out of my due time,**
> **Why should I try to set the crooked straight?**
> **Let it suffice me that my murmuring rhyme**
> **Beats with light wing against the ivory gate,**
> **Telling a tale not too importunate**
> **To those who in the sleepy region stay,**
> **Lulled by the singer of an empty day.**

THE BLUE CLOSET

The decorative and the ornamental side of the Pre-Raphaelite movement are illustrated in this poem. Though there is a thread of narrative upon which the poem is built, its chief interest or appeal is in the vivid treatment of pictorial details. The basic situation which "The Blue Closet" treats is one involving Lady Louise who is in love with Arthur. Arthur rode off one day wearing her scarf, an indication of favor, and he was never heard of again. Then one day Arthur returns, but he returns, as we see at the end of the poem, in the form of a ghost. Arthur leads Lady Louise, her sister, Lady Alice, and their two damsels across a bridge into the land of death. Their song and their wait in the Blue Closet for these many years has ended on Christmas-eve, and the **refrain** ends the poem:

> **And ever the great bell overhead**
> **And the tumbling seas mourned for the dead;**
> **Fro their song ceased, and they were dead.**

"The Blue Closet" is a characteristic escape piece by Morris. It is a poem which creates the mood of mystery and wonder in a medieval setting, and one which is more concerned with ornament and decoration than with narrative. It is a poem which is like a tapestry, and we find here almost lifeless figures who are without any real significance. Morris offers us then in "The Blue Closet" a poem which draws us away from the ugly and drab realities which he saw in Victorian society. It provides a "romantic holiday," as it were, in an imaginative world of an exotic past. Such work on the part of Morris anticipates the "purer" aesthetic verse of Swinburne.

MORRIS AND COMPANY

John Ruskin's chapter on "The Nature of Gothic" in *The Stones of Venice* contrasted the joys of the medieval skilled craftsman building Gothic cathedrals with the drabness of the factory worker in industrial England of the nineteenth century. Ruskin inspired Morris to found Morris and Company in 1861, and here Morris, together with skilled craftsmen, made stained glass windows, tapestries and furniture. He is also the inventor of the Morris chair.

SOCIAL VIEWS

The literary career of William Morris may be safely divided into the years up to 1877 which found him concerned with poetry and painting, and then after 1877 came his period of social concern. Morris, under the influence of Ruskin, believed that the industrial complex of Victorian England was producing things which no one needed, and furthermore he believed that factory workers were being reduced to machines. He thus advocated some form of socialism to replace the society which he believed was de-humanizing man and labor. One should consult his essay "The Art of the People" (1879) to find these views. Shortly after, Morris read the works of Karl Marx and became a communist. His dream was of an ideal society, a Utopia, where men would be allowed to follow a simple life of creative activity and where art would again have a significant influence upon people. In his later prose Morris assumed the role of a Victorian prophet and he renounced the earlier escapism of his poetry of exotic "dreams" to become vitally concerned with the antagonism which exists between the public and the artist.

CONCLUSION

In 1902 William Butler Yeats, the great modern poet (1865-1939), wrote of Morris as "the one perfectly happy and fortunate poet of modern times." Yeats noted that Morris had the ability to create beautiful things without labor, and he continued: "It is as though Nature spoke through him at all times in the mood that is upon her when she is opening the apple-blossom or reddening the apple or thickening the shadow of the boughs, and that the men and women of his verse and of his stories are all the ministers of her mood." These remarks indicate the characteristic richness and pleasure that are to be found in Morris. His poetry is not widely read today, but this is strange because Morris makes a bridge between the Victorian and the Modern periods in poetry. Perhaps his social writings have dwarfed his accomplishments in poetry. At any rate Morris is a very significant poet of the period who offers us something strikingly different, a poetry that is devoid of **didactic** or moral intent. His poetry is one of pure beauty, of imaginative lushness, and of rich pictorial detail. Morris during his life was painter, poet, businessman, designer of furniture, and a political agitator; the variety of his career indicates that he was a man of lofty ideals.

THE VICTORIAN POETS

TEXTUAL ANALYSIS

ALGERNON CHARLES SWINBURNE

....

| INTRODUCTION

If you are inclined to believe that a poetry of "style" can exist independently of content value, then it is still possible to regard Swinburne as an important poet of the nineteenth century. Even in Swinburne's own day it was fairly commonplace to divide his poetry into form and idea, and to praise him for his style and condemn him for his thought, or lack of it. The emphasis in literary criticism in the present generation is away from any dichotomy between form and matter. It is now generally felt that a poem is an integral unit, with each part dependent on, even dictated, by the others. While it is sometimes necessary for the sake of analysis to separate the parts, the critic and reader are aware that this is just a temporary procedure. Any permanent division between the parts, between the so-called **theme** and its expression, which suggests that the two can function independently, is regarded as a denial of the true identity of poetry. But despite this general critical attitude Swinburne is still talked of today as a master of language and rhythms with which he communicates little or nothing of value.

In his own era Swinburne was attacked not because his ideas were thought of as shallow or limited, but because they were considered too revolutionary and shocking. Indeed, Swinburne reacted, in his youth, against much of what is constant in the Victorian sensibility. He rebelled against Christianity not on scientific grounds, but emotional grounds. Rather than bemoaning his loss of faith in Christianity, as did most of his contemporaries, he rejoiced that man was going to be freed from the yoke of a repressive religion. Akin to his rejection of conventional Christian morality was his championship of body and sensual pleasures, at a time when other Victorian poets for the most part ignored the fact that there was a physical basis to love. His active support for the political liberty and equality of peoples, and particularly for the unification of Italy, aroused strong distrust among the increasingly chauvinistic English.

For these reasons and for his rather dissolute personal life as well, Swinbourne was regarded in the years between 1866 and 1879, as the enfant terrible of English poetry. By the time of his death in 1909 he had achieved a certain degree of respectability due to both his changing and the times in which he lived.

EARLY LIFE AND EDUCATION

Swinburne was born in 1837 of a wealthy and aristocratic family. His father was an admiral in the British navy, and his mother was the daughter of an English earl. He attended Eton and then Oxford and distinguished himself as a brilliant student of the classics and Italian and French literature. His nervous temperament and rebellious nature were early apparent, however, and he left Oxford without taking a degree. He then went to London and, supported by a family allowance, he took up a Bohemian existence. Rossetti and the other Pre-Raphaelites were soon among his friends. He shared with them a belief in the importance of "art for art's sake," and the primacy of aesthetic over intellectual values in poetry. He particularly disliked the moralizing of Tennyson and was later to write some clever parodies of his poetry. Swinburne did not believe that poetry should be empty of thought, however, but a powerful agent to move men's minds. He was very fascinated by the Elizabethan age, and felt that this was the greatest period of literature, because its drama was inciting without being overtly **didactic**. His first publication in 1860 was a volume containing two plays *The Queen Mother* and *Rosamund* which were Elizabethan in style, but they passed unnoticed. The Victorians were shy of literature which attempted to imitate the boldness and violence of an age much less genteel than their own.

ATALANTA IN CALYDON

Swinburne's first work to attract any attention was his attempt to reproduce a Greek drama in English, *Atalanta in Calydon*. Published in 1865 it tells of a Calydonian youth named Meleager, the son of Oeneus, King of Calydon, and Althaea, his wife. Oeneus had offended Artemis, the goddess of the hunt, by refusing to offer sacrifices to her. As revenge Artemis sent a wild boar into Calydon which ravished the crops. As the play opens Meleager and the other warriors are preparing to go on a hunt to slay the boar. They are joined by the Arcadians, including Atalanta, an Arcadian maiden who is the virgin priestess of Artemis. Fearful of her son's life, because of a dream she has had, Althaea warns her son to beware of earthly love. Althaea had dreamt at the time of her son's birth that the Fates promised him good fortune until the brand on the hearth burned out. Althaea had promptly quenched the burning brand with her own hands and hidden it. She felt safe about her son's life until she had another dream in which the brand burst into flames, and then Love came and stamped it out. Meleager ridicules his mother's fear of the gods, however, and refuses to believe in their power. On the hunt he is successful in killing the boar, and he gives the spoils to Atalanta, with whom he has fallen in love. Atalanta laughs with joy as she takes the gift, but Meleager's kinsmen think that she is laughing at them. They attack the maiden, and Meleager is forced to kill his two uncles in order to protect her. His mother is distraught over Meleager's deed, and blames his pride and ambition for the death of her brothers. Realizing that the will of the gods is omnipotent and her son's fate cannot be escaped, she throws the brand into the fire where it is at last consumed. As a result of this act Meleager dies. Althaea's dreams have come true. Her son has met his death because of his love for Atalanta. The mother, overcome with sorrow, soon follows him. Artemis has had her revenge on the pride of Oeneus.

Swineburne's emphasis on the conflict between man and his fate, symbolized in the power of the Gods, is imitative of the Greek dramatists. His portrait of Meleager, whose pride and ambition make him think he can control his destiny but which lead to his downfall, is characteristic of classical drama. Swinburne also employs the form of Greek drama, utilizing only a few characters and a chorus, which describes and comments on the action. But his play has none of the concentrated power which comes from the Greek conception of character, which is at once heroic and yet intensely human. As is typical of Swinburne, the dialogue and choral passages are not trimmed to their functional use but bloated and distracting at times. Some of the choruses are usually printed in anthologies and, isolated from the play, still read well. The problem is, as often with Swinburne, that whole passages can be removed from his work and be as meaningful as in their original context.

1866 POEMS AND BALLADS

At the age of twenty-nine Swinburne's relative obscurity as a poet came to an abrupt end. With the publication of *Poems and Ballads* he became both famous and infamous. His book was attacked as obscene, immoral, and blasphemous, and it shocked not only the literary critics but the general public as well. His Victorian readers were not shocked by his rejection of Christianity in itself, but joy the joy he expressed in rejecting it for what seemed to them a religion of carnality. Swinburne's descriptions of perverted sexual love in such lyrics as "Dolores," "Faustine," and "Laus Veneris" were too explicit and detailed to win the favor of the readers of Tennyson's "Queen of the May." If they were "animating," it was certainly not in the manner Arnold had in mind. John Morley, an important critic of the day and one regarded as liberal-minded, summed up much of the public reaction to the poems:

> **And no language is too strong to condemn the mixed vileness and childishness of depicting the spurious passion of a putrescent imagination, the unnamed lusts of sated wantons, as if they were the crown of character and their enjoyment the great glory of life.**

Besides moral indignation Morley's review does suggest some of the defects of Swinburne's lyrics, regarded as art. He complains of the monotonous reiteration of the same words and images:

> This stinging and biting, all these "little lascivious regrets," all this talk of snakes and fire, of blood and wine and brine, of perfumes and poisons and ashes, grows sickly and oppressive on the senses.

Certainly a modern reader who is saturated with much bolder material than that Swinburne offered the public in 1866, can still complain of the lack of variation, of structure and **climax** in these lyrics. The unsparing use of violent **imagery** and ideas dissipates whatever effect Swinburne was trying to achieve by jading the reader's taste to satiety. Moreover, Swinburne shows little honesty in his treatment of passion. He is frank, but reveals no depth of insight into human nature. Baudelaire, whom Swinburne greatly admired, uses some of the same material in order to explore the nature of evil. Swinburne seems often to be using it to titillate himself and the reader.

HYMN TO PROSERPINE

One of the poems in the 1866 volume which offended the public on grounds other than sensuality was the dramatic poem "Hymn to Proserpine." The speaker is an unconverted Pagan who laments the establishment of the Christian faith in Rome (Constantine's Edict of Milan, 313, A.D.), and the outlawing of the pagan religion. Proserpine is the queen of the underworld and therefore of death. The pagan begs her to deliver him from this life now that the Christian religion has robbed it of all the beauty, joy, and creativity it had when man worshipped the pagan deities. Historically, Swinburne is inaccurate in his depiction of the early Christian attitude. One of the reasons Christianity won so many converts was that it taught that man must be joyous and hopeful in the light of Christ's resurrection, which brought eternal life to all men. Whether aware of this or not, Swinburne is more interested in expressing his attitude towards what he regarded as the oppressive, deadening restrictions of Christian morality in nineteenth-century England. Better to be dead, Swinburne thought, than to live a life which denies the fulfillment of one's human instincts and appetites.

The poem is structured on a contrast between the pagan and Christian experiences and reinforced by the symbols and images associated with each in the speaker's mind. The beautiful Apollo, the sun god and patron of music and art, is dethroned as king, by Christ who is his antithesis:

Thou hast conquered, O Pale Galilean; the world has grown grey from they breath....(lines 35-36)

The golden beauty of Apollo has been replaced by the barren greyness of Christ for the speaker. And just as Apollo, the king, has been dethroned, so too Cytherea (Venus), the Queen. Mary, the Virgin Mother, has replaced Cytherea, goddess of sensual love and beauty:

For thine came pale and a maiden, and sister to sorrow; but ours,

Her deep hair heavily laden with odour and colour of flowers....(lines 35 36).

Obviously this poem did not please a generation which thought of the passing of the Christian faith as the greatest calamity the world had yet faced. Swinburne's ability to make pretty music using the fairly uncommon **anapestic** foot (short, short, long) was not enough to pacify their outraged sensibilities.

SONGS BEFORE SUNRISE 1871

Swinburne was not chastened by the public disdain, and he continued to champion revolutionary causes. He became a close friend of Mazzini, the Italian patriot, and devoted himself to helping the movement for Italian freedom. Songs before Sunrise depart from the poet's preoccupation with the flesh, to champion the cause of political liberty.

TO WALT WHITMAN IN AMERICA

One of the most well-known poems from Songs before Sunrise is a eulogy to Wait Whitman. Whitman, the mid-nineteenth century American poet, most famous for his work Leaves of Grass, was similar to Swinburne in certain respects. He wrote a bold, exuberant poetry that championed American democracy and was frank in his use of sexual imagery. Swinburne's poem "To Walt Whitman in America," praises the song of his American contemporary and asks him to inspire the English people with the same love of democracy that he tries to instill in the American people. As in "Hertha," another famous poem in the 1871 volume, Swinburne is blunt in his rejection of any religion but the worship of man. Whitman often spoke of man as being divine, but he did not explicitly claim he was God, as does Swinburne:

> God is buried and dead to us....
> ....
> The soul that is substance of nations
> Reincarnate with fresh generations
> The great god Man, which is God. (Lines 106, 117 - 120)

Swinburne was in revolt against all that was Victorian, but in these similar lines he shows that he is still very much a child of his age. It would be hard to imagine any poet in the twentieth century, after the horror of two world wars, making a similar claim for man.

SWINBURNE'S LATER LIFE AND CAREER

By 1879 Swinburne was in very ill health caused by a nervous disorder and his dissipated mode of life. He was rescued from a total breakdown by Theodore Watts-Dunton, a lawyer, who took the poet to live with him in a villa at Putney. Here Swinburne spent the last thirty years of his life being carefully protected and taken care of by Watts-Dunton. Here Swinburne was transformed from an ardent rebel into a stringent political conformist and champion of British nationalism and imperialism. His repudiation of Walt Whitman is just a sample of his reformation. He continued to write poetry, but it little affects his reputation. His interest in Elizabethan literature grew, and he wrote critical studies of Shakespeare and Ben Jonson, which at least attempted to restore interest in an area of literature neglected by the Victorians. It is difficult to know whether the care of his respectable friend Watts-Dunton helped him to conserve his waning poetic powers, or stifled what was left of them.

CONCLUSION

Swinburne differs from the major Victorian poets in many respects. Not the least of these is his sense of humor. He could laugh at the pretensions and stylistic devices of other poets, and more importantly he could also laugh at himself. "The Higher

Pantheism in a Nutshell," is a refreshing **parody** of Tennyson's "Higher Pantheism," and reduces ambivalences to absurdity. "Nephelidia," also published in 1880, takes to task Swinburne's own love for words, words, words.

In summary, Swinburne is an important figure to read in studying the Victorian literary movement. His poetry, by its very differences, sheds light on the work of his contemporaries and prepares us for the transition to modern poetry. A review of his work shows that Swinburne has more ideas than he is usually credited with. To praise him only as a maker of beautiful words, without any substance, is not really to give him any credit. After all, as Gerard Manly Hopkins said in regard to Swinburne's **diction**, "But words only, are only words." (Letters to Dixon).

THE VICTORIAN POETS

TEXTUAL ANALYSIS

GERARD MANLEY HOPKINS

INTRODUCTION

Gerard Manley Hopkins is a difficult poet to place in the Victorian period. Chronologically his short life spans the second half of the nineteenth century, 1844 - 1889. But Hopkins' poetry was unknown in his own time, except to a very small group of friends. Robert Bridges, the poet friend to whom Hopkins entrusted his poetry upon his death, did not publish an edition of the poems until 1918. Bridges did not make any attempt to bring Hopkins' work to the attention of the public before this time, except for a few pieces included in anthologies, because he felt that the literary taste in general was not ready for this new kind of poetry. Bridges was almost certainly right. It is doubtful that Hopkins' poetry would have been appreciated in the nineteenth century by readers used to the much different tradition of Tennyson, Arnold, Browning, etc. Moreover Hopkins' poetic craft is more similar to such modern poets as Yeats and Eliot than to his Victorian counterparts, and it is easier to consider him in terms of twentieth-century attitudes towards poetry. Because of the relative obscurity of Hopkins' life as a Jesuit priest, his particular genius had the opportunity to develop rather independently of influences on nineteenth century poetry, and, of course, Hopkins never had to cater to the taste of his public, which was non-existent. His poetry, therefore, does not stem from the immediate sources of his age, and it has no influence traceable on the other Victorian poets. In the last thirty years the critical estimate of Hopkins' work has steadily risen. The earlier fascination for his technique has deepened to include a more comprehensive understanding of his thought. He is certainly a very rich, complex, and, on first reading, difficult poet. Some critics criticize him for having a limited range. But if his range is limited, it is also within its limits profound and moving to a degree rarely found in poets, and hardly at all in Victorian poets.

In order to render even superficial justice to Hopkins' poetry, in a review study of this kind, it would be necessary to consider some of his poems in great detail. He is not a writer whom one can dismiss after finding the "meaning" of the poem. The statement "A poem does not mean, it is" never applied to any poet more fully than to Hopkins. Therefore, rather than a general survey of his poetry, the following pages will briefly consider just a few aspects of his craft.

LIFE AND EDUCATION

Hopkins was born near London in 1844, to prosperous and well-educated parents. He was raised in the moderate Anglican religion of his parents, and educated at Highgate School, London, and Balliol College, Oxford. While at Oxford, where the religious controversy of the Oxford movement was still strong, Hopkins converted to Roman Catholicism in 1866, with Newman as his sponsor. After receiving his B.A. from Oxford in 1867, Hopkins decided to enter the Jesuit order to become a priest in 1868. Upon entering the order Hopkins resolved not to write any more poetry and to dedicate himself to the religious life. After seven years he again took up his pen, upon the expressed wish of his superior, and wrote a poem on the wreck of a ship, The Deutschland, in the mouth of the Thames in the winter of 1875. Five Franciscan nuns, exiles from the religious persecution in Germany, were drowned in the disaster. The resulting poem, "The Wreck of the Deutschland," is Hopkins' major long work and a masterpiece. The poem is more than just a powerful imaginative recreation of the experience. It is an exploration of the mystery of evil in the world and its relationship to God's benevolence. Starting with the paradox of the suffering and death of five nuns who have devoted themselves to God, just at the time they are reaching safety, the poet goes on to explore the basic paradoxes of Christianity itself. The poem ends on a triumphant note of affirmation and joy in God's power, which transmutes evil into good, submission into mastery, sacrifice into joy, death into victory.

Hopkins was ordained a priest in 1877 at the age of thirty-three. He spent the remainder of his short life first as a preacher in the Liverpool section of London, then as a lecturer in the classics at the Jesuit college at Oxford, Stonyhurst, and finally as a Professor of Greek at University College, Dublin. He had little time for writing with his heavy burden of priestly and scholarly duties. Writing poetry did not come easily to him, as he was a painstaking craftsman and also suffered severe bouts of nervous depression when his creative efforts seemed futile to him. Besides "The Wreck of the Deutchland" he left only a small collection of lyrics and sonnets. Their **themes** and techniques were clearly adumbrated in the earlier poem. He went on to refine, crystallize, and individuate them in a series of exquisitely wrought pieces.

INSCAPE AND INSTRESS

A brief note on Hopkins' theory of inscape and instress is necessary to an understanding of what he was trying to achieve in his poetry. Duns Scotus, the medieval philosopher, believed that each individual object has a distinctive "form," a quality which distinguishes it from any other individual in its species. This thesis was in contrast to that of Thomas Aquinas, who believed that the matter or substance of each individual was distinct, but its form or pattern was generic, that is, it was shared by all other members of the species or class. Jesuit teaching relies heavily on the teaching of Aquinas, but Hopkins was more influenced by the ideas of Scotus. What Scotus called haecceitas, or "thisness," to differentiate it from the generic quidditas, or "whatness," Hopkins referred to as inscape. The word is of Hopkins' coinage, perhaps suggested by the word landscape, which is a sense-perceived pattern. The prefix "in" suggests that this pattern, or by extension, inner form, is not immediately apprehendable, but requires a searching, a seeing into, to discover the unique identity of a thing. Inscape then can be defined as the special individualizing pattern or form, which can be outwardly apparent or inwardly present, which gives a person, or object, or emotion its particular identity. Instress, or simply "stress" is Hopkins' word for the experience of perceiving the inscape of an object. How then are these related to his theory of poetry? Hopkins believed that a poem was the actualization of the instress of inscape, or, in other words, the capturing of the unique quality of an experience or object so that the reader shares with the artist his penetration into its inner selfhood. Poetry, wrote Hopkins, is:

> ...speech framed to be heard for its own sake and interest even over and above its interest of meaning. Some matter and meaning is essential to it but only as an element necessary to support and employ the shape which is contemplated for its own sake - and therefore the inscape must be dwelt on.

Naturally the task of rendering the distinctive quality of an individual object requires a **diction** and rhythm which are themselves unique in order to capture this distinctiveness. This is why Hopkins' style is so strikingly different from conventional poetic expression in the nineteenth century. He was not trying to be strange for its own sake, but because there was no other way to convey the "inscape" at which he was aiming.

PIED BEAUTY

One of the poems in which Hopkins most completely achieves his aim is the beautiful lyric "Pied Beauty." The word "pied" means variegated, covered with patches or spots of two or more colors. In the first **stanza**, which is a shortened version of the eight-line octave of the sonnet form, the poet describes different objects in nature whose beauty is variegated rather than uniform. "Glory be to God for dappled things," the poet begins, and then illustrates these spotted or mottled things: "For skies of couple-colour as a brinded cow," that is, skies in which the colors are joined together as they are on a streaked or spotted cow. White clouds against the darker blue background would be similar in pattern to the splashes of white on a black or tawny cow. The third line, "For rose-moles all in stipple upon trout that swim," describes the deep pink spots of color on trout which look as if they were applied by stippling, that is by the method by which a painter applies color in dots rather than in lines or solid areas. Certain French Impressionist painters of this period used this method to create pictures in which the pinpoints of color, viewed from a distance, blend together to produce a luminous effect (Pointillism). So too the dots of color on the trout when it is swimming produces a similar shimmering effect. Other things which share this dappled quality are "Fresh-firecoal chestnut-falls," that is, the appearance of the roasted chestnut when it is stripped of its husk; "finches wings," birds, such as the sparrow, whose wings are spotted,; "Landscape plotted and pieced - fold, fallow, and plough," that is an area of farmland that has been divided up into sections, some of it planted, some of it left unseeded, some of it ready for ploughing. Not only the things of nature share a pied beauty, but the things of man also. The tools man uses to work with have a beauty too, a beauty which comes with their functional design, rather than any purposely decorative pattern: "And all trades, their gear and tackle and trim."

In the concluding **stanza**, which corresponds to the sextet of a traditional **stanza** but is only four lines, the poet enlarges and generalizes on his opening statement. Having minutely described several "dappled things" in the opening **stanza**, the poet concludes that all things which share in the constantly changing, variegated kaleidoscope of nature bear witness to the timeless, constant beauty of God!

> **All things counter, original, spare, strange,**
> **Whatever is fickle, freckled (who knows how?)**
> **With swift, slow; sweet, sour; adazzle, dim;**
> **He fathers-forth whose beauty is past change:**
> **Praise him.**

The world in which man lives, which comprehends such a vast variety of contrasts, such an amazing panorama of patterns and designs, is a reflection of its Creator, whose identity encompasses all extremes into a perfect and absolute unity of being. Hopkins possessed a sacramental view of the universe, a view held by many saints of the Church. He saw the world as a revelation, a showing forth, of God's nature. He was vividly aware of the hand of God in all things, not just in the great beauties in Nature or the awesome moments in man's experience. As in this poem, Hopkins saw God's presence in the small, often inconsequential or commonplace objects which make up part of man's daily existence. In a sense then, Hopkins in "Pied Beauty" is expressing his own "inscape" into God's nature. In perceiving the unusual beauty that exists in the most commonplace of objects, Hopkins is able to see deeper into their meaning and realize that they are testimonies to God's nature. If God is the source of such variable beauty, then He not only encompasses it but transcends it.

HOPKINS' POETIC TECHNIQUES

A paraphrase of any of Hopkins' poems is useful for two reasons. One, it may clear up some of the obscurities in the text. Two, and much more important, it makes very plain Hopkins' great gift of expression. For to understand what Hopkins is saying in the poem is not at all to share the experience he is rendering. His thought is not difficult. It lies in the main stream of the Christian tradition. His **imagery** is usually drawn from nature. He writes of the country with which his fellow Englishmen were very familiar, and there is nothing exotic or foreign in his descriptions. What is striking about his **imagery** is its use of vivid detail. He singles out a certain aspect of an object which usually goes unnoticed in the larger picture offered by many poets. In doing so, Hopkins grasps at the very essence of the object. The descriptions in the opening **stanza** of "Pied Beauty" illustrate this. His **metaphors** also make associations that at first may seem so strange as to be paradoxical, but upon further reading substantiate the idea the poet is expressing, and indicate his rare gift for perception of similarities between superficially dissimilar objects. Critics often compare Hopkins' vivid **imagery** to that of Keats, whom Hopkins admired and imitated in his early verse. The intense individuality of Hopkins' experiences and his ability to paint very concrete images are traits of Keats as well. But Hopkins' mature poetry has none of the lush, overripe, self-indulgent quality that sometimes mars the work of the Romantic poet. Hopkins' poetry, despite its nature **imagery**, is really more reminiscent of the great **metaphysical** poets of the seventeenth century, such as John Donne. He has the same ability to yoke together disparate images, building with them line by line until they form an integrated structure which unites them all in an harmonious design. The opening lines of "Pied Beauty" illustrate Hopkins' architectural skill. To compare the coloring of the sky to that of a cow may at first seem a rather homely **simile**. But then we note that cloud patterns in the sky are similar in design to a brindled cow, and, furthermore, this **metaphor** prepares us for the descriptions of the farmland three lines below. Hopkins makes clear that the beauty he is praising is not the majestic scenes of towering mountains or glittering oceans. He is speaking of the beauty that is part of man's everyday working world, the world of gear, tackle and trim. At the end of six lines Hopkins, while seemingly just noting a few objects, has actually encompassed the elements of air, fire, water and earth, the four elements which compose matter, according to the traditional philosophical treatments of it. This underscores Hopkins' **theme** that all matter, everything in the world, gives Glory to its Creator.

More than his **imagery**, however, it is Hopkins' **diction** that makes his poetry unique. The poet once insisted that "life must be conveyed into the work and displayed there, not suggested as having been in the artist's mind." The vitality and movement of Hopkins' **diction** gives his poems this life, and makes them essentially dramatic rather than subjective lyrics. He captures an object or experience in all its individuality and conveys it to the reader with a vocabulary and grammatical structure which intensifies rather than dissipates the effect. Only after he has established a concrete situation does he ask the reader to sympathize with his response to it. This is in contrast to much Romantic and Victorian poetry, which dwells on the artist's feelings without sufficiently motivating the reader to sympathize with the emotion expressed.

Hopkins achieves his terse and compressed expression by many means. Often he will employ a word which has more than one meaning, and the ambiguity will reinforce the resonance of the direct statement. He also uses a word in a multiple function. It will be both a noun and a verb, or a verb and a modifier. He leaves out words which serve only as connectives and add nothing to the impact of the line. He draws upon the riches of local dialect, which is more pictorial than formal speech. The strength and purity of Welsh and Anglo-Saxon appealed to Hopkins, and he often uses the simple, direct native words, or combination of words in place of the more abstract, Latinized vocabulary of cultivated English. All these techniques, and others more subtle, give a sense of immediacy to the poem, in which the reader feels that he too is participating in the moment. Rather than the poet gradually expounding the meaning of the event, its significance almost explodes upon the reader with the same force it has for the artist.

Hopkins' metrical patterns also contribute much to the effectiveness of the poem. He does not employ conventional scansions, but devised his own rhythmical patterns which give him greater flexibility in creating harmonies which reinforce his meanings. He called his metrical system "Sprung Rhythm." The lines have a definite number of stresses, but the number of unaccented syllables is not fixed. This system is not original to Hopkins, but dates back to the Anglo-Saxon mode of scansion. In Hopkins' poems there is a subtle contrapuntal effect created by the counterpointing of the word stress against the sense stress. The basic metrical pattern of the line, its musical base, is fused with the pattern established by the natural speaking voice to create a marked and yet natural rhythm. In this way Hopkins achieves the flexibility which comes usually with the use of **free verse**, and yet retains the musical quality of conventional meters.

CONCLUSION

Such poems as "God's Grandeur," "Spring and Fall," "The Windhover," "Felix Randal," "Henry Purcell," "Carrion Comfort," and indeed all of Hopkins' brief canon illustrate his mastery of the poetic craft. But only by carefully reading and absorbing them into himself can one gain any knowledge of Hopkins' genius. And indeed it is valueless to talk about Hopkins' style as if it can be separated from his content. The two are fused inextricably together in "the achieve of, the mastery of the thing."

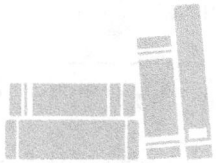

THE VICTORIAN POETS

TEXTUAL ANALYSIS

THE MINOR VICTORIAN POETS

INTRODUCTION

The use of the designation "minor" Victorian poets is not meant to indicate that the achievement of the figures in this chapter is unimportant. Certain of the figures in this chapter might well be considered major figures by another list. Time often establishes the rank of poets, and it is often seen that some poets even become more popular long after their death. The work of Hopkins, for instance, was not published until after his death and has been an important force on modern poetry. So also some might consider the work of George Meredith to be that of a major figure. The student of the period is advised to read these poets with due seriousness, to estimate their individual achievement for himself, and to come to recognize that each had a very real importance, whether that be great or small, in the panorama of the Victorian scene.

ELIZABETH BARRETT BROWNING (1806-1861)

Elizabeth Barrett Browning's poetry was extremely popular during her lifetime, for the noted poetess offered her readers moral counsel and passion for liberal and humanitarian causes. She viewed poetry as a serious art which offered divine wisdom, and her poem "The Dead Pan" lists the subjects for poetry:

> **What is true and just and honest,**
> **What is lovely, what is pure....**
> **O brave poets....**
> **Look up Godward; speak the truth in**
> **Worthy song from earnest soul!**

Her poem "A Musical Instrument" indicates basically the same idea as it describes the poet as a servant of divinity. "On a Portrait of Wordsworth by B.R. Haydon" describes the portrait and the figure of Wordsworth with the same serious attitude toward poetry: "Takes here his rightful place as a poet-priest / By the high altar, singing prayer and prayer / To the higher Heavens." She was a great champion of humanitarian causes such as the abolition of child labor, and her liberal political views led her to work for Italian freedom from Austria. Though an invalid for much of her early life, she found happiness and improved health in the years following her marriage to Robert Browning. Together they lived in Italy until her death in 1861.

SONNETS FROM THE PORTUGUESE

Elizabeth Barrett Browning's reputation is largely based on this series of intimate and autobiographical **sonnets** in which she recorded the stages of her love for her husband. Her other verse is too filled with contemporary problems and her personal political views which are often tediously expounded. Also there is too much overt didacticism in her other work. But in the **sonnets** she found her strength which was the presentation of personal experience. Under the guise or fiction of a translation from the Portuguese, she presents an intimate sequence of **sonnets** which record her feelings during the time that Browning courted her. Perhaps the most famous of these **sonnets** is the forty-third which is quoted in full to reveal the particular flavor of the group:

> **How do I love thee? Let me count the ways.**
> **I love thee to the depth and breadth and height**
> **My soul can reach, when feeling out of sight**
> **For the ends of Being and ideal Grace.**
> **I love thee to the level of everyday's**
> **Most quiet need by sun and candle light.**
> **I love thee freely, as men strive for the Right;**
> **I love thee purely, as they turn from Praise.**
> **I love thee with the passion put to use**
> **In my old griefs, and with my childhood's faith.**
> **I love thee with a love I seemed to lose**
> **With my lost saints - I love thee with the breath,**
> **Smiles, tears, of all my life! - and, if God choose,**
> **I shall but love thee better after death.**

CHRISTINA ROSSETTI (1830-1894)

Christina Georgina Rossetti was born in 1830, the sister of the famous poet and painter Dante Gabriel Rossetti. She was, however, rather remote from the cultural and political turmoil that marked her home. Christina spent a rather simple life caring for relatives and performing other good works. Her poetry reflects a rather simple lyric quality devoid of worldly experience. A deep religious asceticism caused her on two occasions to break off plans for marriage. Christina was a High

Church Anglican, and in the first case her suitor reverted to Roman Catholicism, while in the second case her suitor was not sufficiently interested in religion. Both of these situations caused her much pain, and as a result most of her love lyrics are concerned with frustration and parting. Indeed the dominant **theme** of her poetry is frustration and the feeling that death alone will bring relief. Her poem "Life and Death" opens: "Life is not sweet. One day it will be sweet/To shut our eyes and die;" the opening of the second **stanza** continues this thought: "Life is not good. One day it will be good / To die, then live again."

Christina Rossetti's early work revealed a clear affinity with the aims of the Pre-Raphaelite Brotherhood, and her volume of 1862 titled *Goblin Market and Other Poems* was the first collection in this manner to gain wide recognition. Yet her later work with its characteristic simple lyric gift defies classification. "Song" is a simple lyric where the speaker asks that there be no flowers or sad songs after her death, for "Haply I may remember, /And haply may forget." "After Death" presents a man looking upon the bed of a girl who has just died, and he mutters that she is a poor child. The girl, who is the speaker in the poem, then says: "He did not love me living; but once dead/He pitied me; and very sweet it is/To know he still is warm though I am cold." In summation, Christina Rossetti is a poetess of considerable lyric charm. The simple **diction**, the spontaneous record of personal emotions, and the natural and musical cadences that are to be found in her poetry make her a lyricist deserving note.

GEORGE MEREDITH (1828-1909)

George Meredith was both poet and novelist, and some of his novels are *The Ordeal of Richard Feverel* (1859), *The Adventures of Harry Richmond* (1871), *The Egoist* (1879), and *Diana of the Crossways* (1885). As a poet, his work has suffered undeserved neglect, and it would seem that Meredith deserves more attention. His major work is a sequence of sixteen line **sonnets** titled *Modern Love*, which is really a kind of novel in verse. *Modern Love* is a study in the dissolution of marriage and no doubt derives from Meredith's personal experience. When Meredith was twenty-one and just beginning his career as a man of letters in London, he married the daughter of Thomas Love Peacock, the English satirist. Nine years after their marriage Meredith's wife eloped to Europe with another artist. Thus ended a marriage that was marked by a series of quarrels. He remarried later and this helped to restore a more optimistic tone to his work. The **sonnet** sequence which records a similar experience of marital dissolution is rather loosely connected by a **theme** of progression toward ultimate and tragic collapse. The sequence is somewhat marred, however, by Meredith's tendency to avoid the direct expression of experience and to substitute vague and abstract metaphors.

One can note in Meredith's novels a cool and detached view of human nature, for his novels are rather objective studies in character. In his lyric verse this same objective and detached view prevails as Meredith addresses himself to the problems posed for his age by the clash between Christianity and science. Meredith's philosophy was a naturalistic one, which ruled out ideas of a personal God. Instead Meredith celebrated Earth, nature, and unalterable law which was working in an evolutionary process toward human perfection. Such poems as "Hard Weather" and "The Lark Ascending" reveal both Meredith's philosophical bent and his delight in the physical world of nature.

EDWARD FITZGERALD (1809-1888)

FitzGerald was a retiring, scholarly man who wrote one of the most widely read poems in our literature, *The Rubaiyat of Omar Khayyam of Naishapur*. He attended Cambridge where he became friends with Tennyson and William Makepeace Thackery, the Victorian novelist. His retiring ways led him to a peaceful rural life where he indulged in his scholarly interests and tended his garden. Not even a broken marriage disturbed the calm with which FitzGerald surrounded himself. His interest in Persian led him to Omar Khayyam, a twelfth-century mathematician and astronomer from Naishapur in Persia. Omar's Rubaiyat in quatrains appealed to FitzGerald and he set about to render into English the essential spirit and thought of the Persian. No doubt the epicurean and skeptical tone of the original attracted FitzGerald and in translating the Persian he used what has been called the "FitzGerald stanza." The following quotation should illustrate this:

> **Come, fill the Cup, and in the fire of Spring**
> **Your Winter-garment of Repentance fling;**
> **The Bird of Time has but a little way**
> **To flutter - and the Bird is on the Wing.**

It will be noted that in this **stanza** the third line does not **rhyme** but has the effect of hovering there and offering a certain lyrical delicacy to the stanza.

In the Rubaiyat of FitzGerald there is an obvious epicurean philosophy of enjoyment of the moment of time and pleasure. The rich cadences of the poem and the Oriental **imagery** offer a rich experience of haunting loveliness. Mixed with this epicurean thought is a melancholy hedonism that helped to shape the moral incertitude of the late nineteenth century. The poem is deservedly quoted often, for such memorable lines as follow:

> **A Book of Verses underneath the Bough,**
> **A Jug of Wine, a Loaf of Bread - and Thou**
> **Beside me singing in the Wilderness -**
> **Oh, Wilderness were Paradise enow!**

FitzGerald also wrote *Euphranor* (1851), a prose dialogue containing his meditations, and his letters are quite interesting in their presentation of his singular personality. He also made paraphrases from Greek and Spanish, the best of which is *Such Stuff as Dreams Are Made Of*, from Calderon's *Six Dramas of Calderon*.

ARTHUR HUGH CLOUGH (1819-1861)

Clough, whose name **rhymes** with "rough," reveals many of the intellectual and religious uncertainties that beset the Victorian Period. He was influenced by his mother's pious beliefs and later while at Rugby School by the Liberal Protestantism of Thomas Arnold. While at Oxford, Clough encountered the claim of Newman's Oxford Movement and Anglo-Catholicism, and the counter claims of science and Biblical criticism. Clough was forced to think through these problems for himself and he emerged a skeptic, that is, one suspending judgment. In 1848 he resigned his fellowship at Oxford because he believed he could not subscribe to the doctrines of the Church of England. Much of his life was spent in travel and in different educational positions.

Clough's first volume of poetry is titled *The Bothie of Tober-na-Vuolich* (1848), a delightful undergraduate love story in verse. Another lengthy poem is *Dipsychus* (1850) and the hero's name of the title means "two-souled," which refers to the split between his worldliness and his idealism. Dipsychus is like Faust in that he converses with a spirit which is his own worldly common sense, and in the end he submits to the world with an accompanying sense of regret for the loss of his ideals. In Clough's "The Latest Decalogue" there is biting **satire** of the standards of bourgeois society with its professed adherence to religious commandments:

> **Bear not false witness; let the lie**
> **Have time on its own wings to fly:**
> **Thou shalt not covet, but tradition**
> **Approves all forms of competition.**

Sonnet 4 from *Seven Sonnets on the Thought of Death* treats the conflict between a mechanistic universe and the human longing for religious faith. Some had chosen blindly to cling to the larger hope of belief, but Clough asks if this is not like the bird's "Burying her eyesight." The question raised is whether belief is not self-willed, a wishful longing that ignores facts.

"Qua Cursum Ventus" takes its title from Virgil's Aeneid, Bk. III, lines 268-269, and they may be translated: "As the wind blows, so the vessel takes its due course." Clough's poem treats two ships that are tossed on the seas and go on their journeys separately, but in the end it is hoped they are joined:

> **One port, methought, alike they sought,**
> **One purpose hold where'er they fare,**
> **O bounding breeze, O rushing seas!**
> **At last, at last, unite them there!**

There is a personal background to the poem and this involves the separation between the poet and his friend, W.G.

Ward, a friend while at Oxford who had become a Roman Catholic. Clough held a vague theism, and the poem can thus be interpreted in the light of the personal separation of religious views. Yet there is more universal meaning in the experience, for differences in beliefs are common. "Qui Laborat, Orat" ("He who works, prays") suggests that vocal prayer to the Divine may be too bold, and instead a life of work in service of man may truly be a better form of praise and devotion.

Clough is always linked with Matthew Arnold for both were friends and both have much in common. Yet Arnold in his poem Thyrsis took issue with Clough's choice of an easier position, namely the skeptic's. Arnold became impatient with Clough's indecisiveness, and wrote in Thyrsis: "It irk'd him to be here; he could not rest." Clough, though, treated the deep problems of his age with due seriousness in his poetry and he wrote philosophical lyrics of considerable merit. In his own time, Arnold and others claimed there was no "art" or "beauty" in Clough, but today we can more readily accept the sincerity, the realistic speech, and the avoidance of classical and medieval legends in Clough.

WILLIAM ERNEST HENLEY (1849-1903)

Henley suffered throughout his life from tuberculosis and his poetry reflects the constant struggle against pain and suffering. He revolted against mid-Victorian attitudes and stressed individuality and defiance in the face of the battle between life and death. Henley was one of the first writers to praise the tragic gloom of Thomas Hardy's work. He is also the real founder of **free verse**, that is verse without any regular metrical pattern and usually without **rhyme**. Henley's "In Hospital" is a series of poems written during his confinement in Edinburgh Infirmary and it presents a strongly realistic portrait of accurately observed sights and sounds in a large hospital:

> A square, squat room (a cellar on promotion),
> Drab to the soul, drab to the very daylight;
> Plasters astray in unnatural-looking tinware;
> Scissors and lint and apothecary's jars.

The **realism** of "In Hospital," as illustrated in the above quotation from the poem "Waiting," is countered in Henley by a strong romanticism. One of his most famous and most frequently anthologized poems is "Invictus," or Unconquered. In this poem there is a Byronesque devotion to the Strong Man, the man of force and defiance. Very familiar to readers is the last stanza of "Invictus:"

Equally romantic in its picture of a peaceful death is "I.M. Margaritae Sorori" (To the Memory of Sister Margaret). This poem reminds one of certain lines in Keats's "Ode to a Nightingale" and in Shelley's "**Stanzas** Written in Dejection, near Naples."

FRANCIS THOMPSON (1859-1907)

Francis Thompson was the son of Roman catholic converts and he himself hoped to enter the priesthood. However, he was not considered eligible; he later also failed to complete medical studies. Thompson then lived the life of a tramp in London where poverty was his lot. Addiction to opium led to the destruction of his health. In 1888 Wilfred Meynell, an editor of a Catholic magazine, and his wife Alice rescued Thompson and recognized his talents. Ill health prevented Thompson from writing extensively, but his work marks him as a noteworthy religious poet. His most famous poem is "The Hound of Heaven," which records the spiritual paradox of man's flight from God and his pursuit of divine love. The rhythm of the poem effectively suggests the speed of flight and pursuit as the opening lines will illustrate:

> **I fled Him, down the nights and down the days;**
> **I fled Him, down the arches of the years;**
> **I fled Him, down the labyrinthine ways**
> **Of my own mind; and in the mist of tears**
> **I hid from Him, and under running laughter.**

Thompson's poetry is akin in spirit to the seventeenth century religious verse of Richard Crashaw and reveals the **metaphysical** fondness for elaborate conceit, paradox, and **imagery**. *Sister Songs* (1895) and *New Poems* (1897) are other collections by Thompson, who also wrote an essay on Shelley who was his favorite poet. Thompson, however worked fitfully, and his end was quickened by consumption and drug addiction. "The Kingdom of God" is the greatest of his poems published posthumously.

EDWARD LEAR (1812- 1888)

The general view of the Victorian Period to later generations is one of gloom and undue seriousness; yet from the time of Charles Dickens' *Pickwick Papers* on there was a flourishing activity in humorous verse and prose. One of the forms of humor used during the period was nonsense verse, a mode of composition used in our own time by James Thurber, the American humorist. Nonsense verse is a form of light verse which entertains because of its strong rhythmic quality and it lacks logical development of thought. Also new words-really nonsense words-are often coined in the poem. One of the chief writers of this type of verse was Edward Lear, a landscape painter who spent a good deal of his life in Mediterranean countries. His *Book of Nonsense* published in 1846 was a collection of limericks for children. Although Lear did not invent the limerick, he did a good deal to popularize its use. Perhaps the following example will indicate the limerick type of nonsense verse:

There was a young man in Iowa
Who exclaimed, "Where on earth shall I stow her!"
Of his sister he spoke, who was felled by an Oak
Which abound in the plains of Iowa.

Lear's two most famous poems are "The Owl and the Pussy-Cat" and "The Jumblies".

LEWIS CARROLL (1832-1898)

Lewis Carroll was the pseudonym of Charles Lutwidge Dodgson, a deacon in the Anglican Church and lecturer in mathematics at Oxford. *Alice in Wonderland* (1865) and *Through the Looking-Glass* (1871) were both addressed to children and have remained among the classics of children's literature. They were written to amuse Dodgson's little girl-friends and they reveal a unique and inimitable distorted logic contrived by an ingenious mathematician. Adults have also delighted in these books, and certain critics have offered elaborate psychological explanations of them. Throughout the two books there are various songs which are parodies at times, but more often are nonsense verse. "Jabberwocky", in *Through the Looking-Glass*, Chapter 1, is an outstanding example of the nonsense writer's fondness for puzzles and intricate word games. Carroll's other writings include *The*

Hunting of the Snark (1876), a narrative poem of fantasy, and *Sylvie and Bruno* (1899-1893).

THE AESTHETIC MOVEMENT

The idea of "art for art's sake" which was a central part of the Aesthetic Movement was in part a reaction against the moral earnestness of the Victorian writers Thomas Carlyle and John Ruskin. One of the great influences upon the movement was Walter Pater, critic and essayist, whose work The Renaissance inspired a reaction against utilitarian and moral conceptions of art. Thus art for the aestheticians of the 1890's meant art for the sake of the pleasure and sensations that it could offer with no reference to any standard of morality or utility. The writers of the period were very conscious of their end of century position and adopted a kind of fashionable and sophisticated pose of weariness and hostility to the drabness of society. They are in a great degree throwbacks to the Romantic Movement and to the poetry of John Keats, for one can notice in their verse the same cultivation of sensation in **imagery**. Despite many shortcomings, the aesthetic credo of the 1890's is responsible in many ways for fostering the idea of the independence of the literary work with its own values and standards which is so much a part of modern criticism.

OSCAR WILDE (1856-1900)

Oscar Fingall O'Flahertie Wills Wilde was born in Dublin, the son of a distinguished surgeon and a minor poetess. He was educated at Trinity College and at Magdalen College, Oxford. Wilde was early noted for his brilliant wit and conversation, his peculiar behavior, and his sympathy with the aesthetic movement. He was influenced by Pater, Rossetti, Swinburne, and the French poet Charles Baudelaire. Gilbert and Sullivan in Patience (1881) satirized Wilde and the earlier Pre-Raphaelite Movement. His first book of Poems was published in 1881, and in 1891 *The Picture of Dorian Gray*. However Wilde's greatest success was as a dramatist, and he is remembered today for such plays as *Lady Windermere's Fan* (1892), *A Woman of No Importance* (1893), *An Ideal Husband* (1895), and *The Importance of Being Earnest* (1895), all delightful social comedies revealing Wilde's characteristic wit.

The fall of Oscar Wilde took place in 1895 when the Marquis of Queensbury accused Wilde of homosexuality. Wilde defended himself against the charge but lost. He was imprisoned for two years under a law of 1885 that made homosexuality a criminal offense. Needless to say public reaction against Wilde was strong, and the aesthetic movement suffered a decline with such writers as William Henley offering a more virile poetry. *The Ballad of Reading Gaol* and the autobiographical *De Profundis* were written as a result of Wilde's experiences in prison. He died three years after his release from prison, an exile living under an assumed name in France. In such poems as "Impression du Matin", "Helas" and "E Tenebris", Wilde reveals his imitations of Swinburne and Rossetti.

ERNEST DOWSON (1867-1900)

Ernest Dowson read widely in French and classical literatures and spent a good part of his youth in France. He attended Oxford briefly but did not pursue a regular academic program leading to a degree. Together with Lionel Johnson and W. B. Yeats he was a member of the Rhymers' Club. His volume *Verses* appeared in 1896. A dissolute life and excessive drinking hastened Dowson's end. His poetry is indebted to the influences of Swinburne, Latin lyric poetry, and French poetry. In "Cynara" Dowson used the alexandrine (iambic hexameter) in a six line **stanza**; the poem reveals the haunting cadence, and the pursuit of sensation that were common among the members of the aesthetic movement:

> Last night, ah, yesternight, betwixt her lips and mine
> There fell thy shadow, Cynara! thy breath was shed
> Upon my soul between the kisses and the wine;
> And I was desolate and sick of an old passion,
> Yea, I was desolate and bowed my head:
> I have been faithful to thee, Cynara! in my fashion.

LIONEL JOHNSON (1867-1902)

Lionel Pigot Johnson was a slight man of five feet, three inches, who received his education at Winchester and Oxford. Johnson rebelled against the military tradition of his father's family to pursue a literary career. He became a member of the Century Guild, a society to promote artistic craftsmanship, and later he joined the Rhymers' Club. In 1891 Johnson became a member of the Roman Catholic Church. Later in 1893 he became an ardent champion of Ireland's political cause. His death came when a sudden stroke caused him to fall off a stool in a London bar; this end was somehow an appropriate end to a life of desperation. In "The Dark Angel" Johnson reveals the torment of the dual nature of his spirit, for, like Wilde, he was a practicing homosexual; the poem examines the efforts of Satan to pervert love:

> Dark Angel, with thine aching lust
> To rid the world of penitence:
> Malicious Angel, who still dost
> My soul such subtile violence!

The poem closes on a note of triumph in the rejection of evil:

**Do what thou wilt, thou shalt not so,
Dark Angel! triumph over me:
Lonely, unto to the Lone I go;
Divine, to the Divinity.**

The particular virtues of Johnson's verse that have called for praise are the sense of order and the feeling for verbal craftsmanship. Other noteworthy poems by Johnson are "The Precept of Silence", and "Mystic and Cavalier".

SUMMARY

The major figures of Victorian literature reveal many of the traits that have been generally associated with the term Victorian. Each, however, to varying degrees modifies our understanding of the term. When we turn to the minor poets, we note also a considerable range and variety. Each of the minor poets has a peculiar and individual fascination, and it is only through a consideration of their achievement that one can come to a deep knowledge of the Victorian Period. In their work one can notice the reaction against the moral earnestness of the Period. With Wilde, Johnson, and Dowson the Victorian Period comes to an end, and the Aesthetic Movement ushers in a different attitude toward the aims and ends of art.

THE VICTORIAN POETS

ESSAY QUESTIONS AND ANSWERS

Question: Discuss Tennyson's treatment of the classical figure Ulysses.

Ulysses was the hero of Homer's *Odyssey*. After fighting in the Trojan war for ten years, his return to Ithica was delayed by a series of fantastic adventures. Once he had finally achieved his destination and was reunited with his wife, Penelope, and his son, Telemachus, Ulysses was content to rule over his peaceful kingdom, happy that his travels were over. Tennyson's poem presents Ulysses as an aged man, no longer the virile warrior of Homer's work. The source of Tennyson's presentation was probably Book XXVI of Dante's *Inferno*, where Ulysses is depicted as dissatisfied with his life and anxious to go on another voyage. So too, Tennyson's dramatic monologue presents Ulysses as its speaker at the moment when he is saying farewell to his family and urging his men to follow him on another voyage. The aged king does not know where his journey will lead him or what dangers may be in store for him, but he

does know that a life spent in striving is better than one that achieves contentment. For there is always some higher goal to pursue. As Ulysses urges on his men to set sail, he tells them, "'Tis not too late to seek a newer world."

Tennyson's portrait of Ulysses, although set in classical times, is very Victorian in its sentiment. The Greek ideal was one of moderation, never to strive for more than one could achieve. But for Tennyson's hero the act of striving, the constant search, the neverending struggle become more important than any goal that is actually achieved. Once one aim is secured there is always a higher one to take its place. This faith in the ability of man to struggle continuously towards greater progress in the future can be interpreted as the logical extension of Darwin's theory of evolution into the spiritual realm. Thus, even if deprived of a belief in the perfection of the afterlife by the doubt raised by science, Tennyson and his contemporaries could cling, somewhat fitfully, to a belief in the future but inevitable perfectibility of man.

"Ulysses" is one of Tennyson's most artistically successful poems. The use of the classical legend provides an objective distancing for the sentiment, which makes it more digestible than a subjective outpouring of emotion. The imagery is particularly impressive in reinforcing the ideas stated in the poem. Ulysses describes himself in terms of a rusted sword which has grown useless from inactivity. This metaphor carries through the suggestion that life is a battle in which the struggle never ceases without bringing defeat. The coming of night implies the coming of Ulysses' death, and his search beyond the sunset implies his search for an afterlife. But until death ends his journey, his determination must be, "To strive, to seek, to find, and not to yield."

Question: Discuss one of the important aspects of Browning's contribution to Victorian literature.

Robert Browning is today best remembered for the series of rich character portraits found in his series of dramatic monologues. From the start of his poetical career Browning had enunciated an aesthetic credo for poetry that was essentially dramatic in principle. His experiences as a dramatist, though highly unsuccessful, helped to sharpen his powers for the writing of dramatic monologues. Early works such as "Pippa Passes" and "Porphyria's Lover" reveal Browning's interest in the dramatic nature of poetry and in the rich opportunities that character study offered. This answer will treat "My Last Duchess" as an example of the dramatic monologue.

As a literary form the dramatic monologue really goes back to the Sonnets of Shakespeare and to the seventeenth-century metaphysical verse of John Donne. T.S. Eliot, in our own century, has written poetry of this type; one example would be "The Love Song of J. Alfred Prufrock". Indeed modern critical theory has emphasized the dramatic nature of all lyric verse. The dramatic monologue is a poem spoken by one person to another whose presence is felt throughout the poem. This second person simply acts as audience and does not speak. The chief concern of the monologue is the revelation of character and motivation at a moment of choice or crisis. Thus the dramatic monologue is a particularly appropriate form for the examination of the soul of man at moments of self-revelation.

"My Last Duchess" is set in the town of Ferrara during the Renaissance, and the poem begins with the Duke of Ferrara speaking to the Count's envoy. It may be noted that Browning was very fond of Italian Renaissance subjects for his poetry. In the poem the Duke describes a painting of his former wife, and we come to learn that she was flirtatious and not attentive to her husband. She failed to take sufficient pride in the Duke's nine-hundred year old name; all leads to the fact that the Duke had her murdered. The Duke states that he refused to stoop. At the close of the poem he descends the staircase with the envoy and discusses his proposed marriage to the Count's daughter. The Duke speaks with a tone of irony in the poem and adopts a casual and cold stance in the face of what he has done. This latter fact has led readers to pronounce unfavorable judgments on the Duke; some have thought him a cold-blooded tyrant who has had his innocent wife murdered. Yet the characteristic complexity of Browning's character studies would point to a more balanced view of the Duke. Though the Duke may certainly be a villain, yet his wife is not all saint. It is the very complexity of the human situation that Browning here illustrates; moral judgment of the characters is suspended before the tensions and uncertainties which the poem probes.

In conclusion, then, it is in the gallery of portraits that Browning presents that we find his true power as a poet. This answer has treated "My Last Duchess", but other poems such as "Andrea del Sarto" and "Fra Lippo Lippi" also illustrate this aspect of Browning. The interest in psychological realism and in human motivation may then be considered one of Browning's major contributions to Victorian literature. Browning's realism in language and also in characterization was part of his larger attempt to explore in his age the problem of how poetry should be written.

Question: How does **imagery** contribute to the total effect of "Andrea del Sarto"?

"Andrea del Sarto" is a dramatic monologue which treats as subject a "faultless painter." Throughout the poem the reappearance of certain colors becomes important for the total meaning and effect of the poem. Grey become an image or symbol for the drabness of Andrea's life, and it is contrasted to the gold of Leonardo and Michaelangelo. Lucrezia, Andrea's wife, is largely responsible for Andrea's failure, for she does not understand his work and is unsympathetic to it. Andrea, however, dotes on his wife and becomes a willing victim to her destructive charms. Her golden hair becomes symbolic of the only "gold" which Andrea ever succeeded to attain, but gold in this sense is a false value. The literal use of gold toward the end of the poem points up that the gold Andrea sought is money, which he needed to satisfy Lucrezia. Thus gold is used as an image suggestive of the true greatness in art attained by Leonardo, Michaelangelo, and Raphael, and it is also used in the literal sense to suggest the materialistic and mundane achievement of Andrea. The ironic contrast is between Lucrezia's "golden hair" and the gold of great art. Andrea's line "A common greyness silvers everything" is suggestive of his paintings and particularly their backgrounds. Twi-light, autumn, and silver-grey suggest the mediocrity of Andrea's life and of his work. His misuse of the French King's gold reveals Andrea's loss of the proverbial golden opportunity, which was destroyed to please Lucrezia with a new house. Toward the end of the poem he asks Lucrezia to allow him to sit the "grey remainder of the evening out", and it is this reality which is juxtaposed for moments against the dreams of greatness. All, however, ends in acceptance of Lucrezia.

Question: Arnold's verse has been called a "poetry of desolation." Discuss the validity of this statement, supporting your answer with examples from his work.

Much of Arnold's poetry is concerned with the spiritual loneliness and despair of modern man. Over and over again Arnold voices the sentiments of the individual who finds himself living in an alien and hostile society in which he can find no peace or contentment. Devoid of the hope which stems from strong religious faith, the poet cannot reconcile himself to the materialistic and ephemeral goals of an industrialized society. Unable to relate to his contemporaries who pursue lives empty of any spiritual goals, he feels himself alone and unaided in his struggle to maintain a life of the spirit.

In his earlier poems, such as "The Forsaken Merman," and the series entitled "Switzerland" and addressed to Marguerite, the loss of personal love causes the poet to feel a sense of desolation and despair. In these poems the sea becomes a symbol of the division between the lovers, which can never be healed because it is occasioned by a deep sense of moral duty rather than any personal vacillation on the part of one or both parties. In "To Marguerite," for example, the poet writes that, "We mortal millions live alone." He compares the lot of human beings to that of islands which are isolated from each other by the surrounding water but which were once part of the same continent. So too the poet and his loved one were once united, but they share the fate of all humanity and are for ever separated by, "The unplumbed, salt, estranging sea."

In "The Buried Life" Arnold writes of the loneliness and feeling of futility which overcomes man even in the midst of his search for happiness in the crowded whirl of social activity which makes up his day. Once again Arnold uses water as a symbol. This time it is the buried stream of the individual's true identity, which he must plumb in order to reach its source. Only when man refuses to benumb himself "with the thousand nothings of the hour," and pursues the quest of his inner self will he find some answer to the meaning of existence.

In "Philomela" Arnold employs the symbol of the nightingale to represent the eternal flight from pain which characterizes man's life. After Philomela had taken revenge on her husband for the rape of her sister Procne, she was turned into a nightingale. But as the poet listens to the song of the bird he hears in it a burst of pain. He realizes that man can never escape the passion and pain which is his doom, just as the nightingale, the "wanderer from a Grecian shore," after all these centuries and in far off places, still reminds man of the ancient legend of "wild, unquenched, deep-sunken, old-world pain."

"The Scholar Gypsy" also tells the legend of a wanderer, but in this poem the wanderer is not fleeing from life, but searching for its hidden meaning. A seventeenth-century Oxford student, born "Before this strange disease of modern life" deprived man of his courage and intellectual curiosity, joined a band of gypsies to discover their secret learning. The poet thinks of the student as immortal because his quest in life was spiritual rather than material. He searches for traces of him among the Oxford environs, but then begs the spirit of the scholar to fly lest it become infected with the mental strife of modern life and so die. In this poem the gypsy scholar who purposely chooses a life isolated from society is blest, while modern man is left desolate by the feverish but sterile contact of others.

The symbol of the gypsy scholar is explored again in Arnold's elegy on the death of Arthur Clough, "Thyrsis." The poet finds meaning and value in Clough's life in that he followed the path of the gypsy scholar and fled the contagion of modern life to pursue his truth. Probably no poem so well expresses Arnold's feeling of desolation as "Dover Beach." Here as in his other poems Arnold holds out some comfort to be found in love and the pursuit of truth. But even more strongly than in "The Buried Life" or "Thyrsis" the hope expressed seems faint in comparison to the forces of destruction combining against it. The last image in the lyric is one of bleak despair over man's fate; the poet compares it to that of an army left stranded as night descends, left without aid and without hope, and ignorant of what the fight for survival is all about.

Question: What was the Pre-Raphaelite Brotherhood and who were some of its outstanding figures?

The Pre-Raphaelite Movement was founded in 1848 as a reaction against the prevailing attitudes and practices in Victorian art. Dante Gabriel Rossetti headed the movement which sought a return to the simplicity and close adherence to nature which was to be found in Italian art prior to Raphael. In large part the movement escaped the ugly world of Victorian industrial society and sought refuge in the romantic climate of medieval and supernatural subjects. The writers in the movement employed sensuous language and detail, heightened imagery, a concentration on pictorial and musical elements, and symbolism. Experiments with meter and rhythm were a part of their larger effort to free their work from convention, rules, and artificial effects. Their aim was to copy the beauty of nature with unswerving truth to the minutest detail. The association of the movement with the pictorial arts makes for a poetry that constantly reveals what has been called a "plastic effect" in Rossetti.

Dante Gabriel Rossetti was both a poet and painter, who had been influenced greatly by the work of Dante, Keats, Scott, and the medieval romances of Thomas Malory. He was also especially attracted to the beauty of woman and the idea of an elevated, spiritual love. His marriage to Elizabeth Siddal proved the disappointment of Rossetti's ideal, and later his love for Jane Morris, the wife of William Morris, offered him renewed hope in this ideal. In Rossetti's sonnet sequence *The House of Life* the subjects of love, life and death are treated. Perhaps Rossetti's "The Blessed Damozel" will serve to illustrate the major features of Rossetti's poetic style and practice. This poem was first published in *The Germ*, a short-lived magazine started in 1850 by the Pre-Raphaelite Brotherhood. The basic situation of the poem involves a lover who gazes up at heaven in a reverie and imagines that he sees his dead loved one. The poem is written in a six line stanza of alternating iambic tetrameter and trimeter. Ten years have passed since the death of the girl, but she in heaven feels that it has been but a day since she joined God's choristers. The contrast between earthly sorrow and heavenly joy is apparent. However, the true appeal of "The Blessed Damozel" lies in its opulent and sensuous description of the damsel who leans from out heaven; the poem relies for its effect upon imagery that appeals to the pictorial imagination. The gown of the girl, the white rose on her gown which symbolizes virginity, the souls passing to heaven like thin flames, and her hair caressing his face are described in sensuous terms which make for a vivid appeal. Rossetti's "Sister Helen" reveals his interest in medieval subject matter.

William Morris was a man of extraordinary talents and interests. In his lifetime, Morris was a poet, architect, businessman, and political propagandist. Early in life, and largely influenced by John Ruskin's *The Stones of Venice*, Morris pursued a passionate interest in things medieval. In 1856 he met Dante Gabriel Rossetti and became a disciple and member of the Pre-Raphaelite Brotherhood. It was under the influence of Rossetti that Morris directed his energies toward painting and poetry. His *The Defense of Guenevere and Other Poems* is one of the finest volumes produced by the Pre-Raphaelites. "The Haystack in the Floods" is set in medieval times and is a ballad revealing the exotic and romantic nature of Morris. *The Earthly Paradise* is a very lengthy poem based on legends and reveals Morris in the Apology as "the idle singer of an empty day". "The Blue Closet" is illustrative of the ornamental and decorative side of the movement. The narrative thread in the poem is slight and relatively unimportant as it treats of Lady Louise and Arthur who returns at the end of the poem to lead the ladies across the bridge into the land of death. In the poem we see the mysterious and supernatural elements pictured effectively to create a mood piece that reminds one of figures on a tapestry. "The Blue Closet" then is one more instance of the Pre-Raphaelites to withdraw from the drabness of Victorian society and the ugly realities which these writers felt surrounded them. It is a poem which seeks to create a mood of mystery and romance set in an exotic time that the poets believed offered them opportunities to capture the true essence of beauty in all its details. The poetry of Rossetti and Morris differs from the social, political, and religious probings that one finds in much of Tennyson, Browning and Arnold. They are important in that they offer us something different, something which anticipates the Aesthetic Movement of the 1890's with its emphasis on "art for art's sake."

Question: Why are the minor Victorian poets important to our understanding of the Victorian Period?

The tendency to offer simple definitions and neat patterns that one so often confronts in textbooks may well be of some help in an attempt to understand the Victorian Period in literature. However all definitions are by nature not complete statements of all the facts, and thus a knowledge of the minor Victorian poets makes us realize the range and variety of experiences that they bear witness to. Thus to say that the period is without humor is offset by our knowledge of Edward Lear and Lewis Carroll with their nonsense verse. George Meredith enriches our understanding of the clash between science and religion, which is so often spoken about in Tennyson and Arnold. A knowledge of the relationship between Arthur Hugh Clough and Matthew Arnold helps to illuminate both of their positions. The exotic and the oriental are revealed in the work of Edward FitzGerald, an author whose life is fascinating in its detachment from mundane and political concerns. When we come to the end of the century, it would be impossible to understand the age without a knowledge of the Pre-Raphaelite Movement and the later Aesthetic Movement of the 1890's. The Aesthetic Movement with such fascinating figures as Oscar Wilde, Ernest Dowson, and Lionel Johnson, presents a strong reaction against the Victorian conception of art and literature. We see in the 1890's the attempt to break from utilitarian and didactic approaches to literature that characterized much of the major achievement of the period. In general a study of the minor figures provides us with a total picture, one that comprehends the tensions and complexities of an age as revealed in the imaginative literature of that age.

THE VICTORIAN POETS

BIBLIOGRAPHY & GUIDE TO FURTHER RESEARCH

SELECTED READINGS IN THE VICTORIAN PERIOD

General Studies

Jerome Buckley, *The Victorian Temper*, 1951.

Walter E. Houghton, *The Victorian Frame of Mind 1830-1870*, 1957.

D. C. Somervell, *English Thought in the Nineteenth Century*, 1929.

G. M. Young, *Victorian England: Portrait of an Age*, 1936.

Studies Of Victorian Literature

Joseph Warren Beach, *The Concept of Nature in Nineteenth-Century English Poetry*, 1936.

Oliver Elton, *A Survey of English Literature, 1780-1880*, 4 vols., 1920, vols. III and IV are very good general guides.

G. H. Ford, *Keats and the Victorians*, 1944.

Graham Hough, *The Last Romantics*, 1949.

E. D. H. Johnson, *The Alien Vision of Victorian Poetry*, 1952.

F. L. Lucas, *Ten Victorian Poets*, 1940.

Robert Langbaum, *The Poetry of Experience*, 1957.

Vida Scudder, *Social Ideals in English Letters*, 1923.

Basil Willey, *Nineteenth Century Studies*, 1949.

Austin Wright, ed., *Victorian Literature: Modern Essays in Criticism*, 1961.

Alfred, Lord Tennyson

W. H. Auden, *A Selection from the Poems of Alfred Lord Tennyson*, 1944. One of the outstanding poets of our time wrote the introduction to this volume in which he emphasizes the anti-Victorian side of Tennyson's personality.

Paull F. Baum, *Tennyson Sixty Years After*, 1948. Baum presents an unsympathetic account.

Jerome H. Buckley, *Tennyson: The Growth of a Poet*, 1961. This recent book by an outstanding scholar attempts to correct the hostile approaches to Tennyson. It is very worthwhile reading.

Sir Harold Nicolson, *Tennyson*, 1923. An important book that gives a somewhat distorted view of the poet's achievement.

Sir Charles Tennyson, *Alfred Tennyson*, 1949. An excellent biography.

Robert Browning

G. K. Chesterton, *Robert Browning*, 1903. Though somewhat dated this book provides a shrewd assessment.

W. C. De Vane, *Browning Handbook*, 1935. A valuable collection of factual information, dates, and sources.

W. Hall Griffin and H. C. Minchin, *The Life of Robert Browning*, 2nd ed. revised, 1938. The standard biography.

Roma A. King, *The Bow and the Lyre*, 1957. Treats the dramatic monologues.

Robert Langbaum, *The Poetry of Experience*, 1957. Discusses Browning's monologues in their relation to modern literature.

Betty Miller, *Robert Browning. A Portrait*, 1952. A biography that is psychological in its approach.

William O. Raymond, *The Infinite Moment*, 1950. An important discussion of Browning's thought.

Matthew Arnold

E. K. Brown, *Representative Essays of Arnold*, 1936. Contains a valuable introduction.

W. Stacy Johnson, *The Voices of Matthew Arnold*, 1961. An important study of Arnold's poetry.

William Robbins, *The Ethical Idealism of Matthew Arnold*, 1959. This book treats Arnold's prose.

Stuart P. Sherman, *Matthew Arnold*, 1917. A general biographical and critical study.

C. B. Tinker and H. F. Lowry, *The Poetry of Matthew Arnold: A Commentary*, 1940. This is a useful handbook.

Lionel Trilling, *Matthew Arnold*, 1949. The best critical study of Arnold.

Dante Gabriel Rossetti

Sir Maurice Bowra, *The Romantic Imagination*, 1949. Bowra's chapter "The House of Life" is an important comment.

Oswald Doughty, *A Victorian Romantic: Dante Gabriel Rossetti*, 1949. A recent and exhaustive biography of the poet.

Graham Hough, *The Last Romantics*, 1949. Contains a valuable chapter on Rossetti.

Gaylord Le Roy, *Perplexed Prophets*, 1953, Chapter VI treats Rossetti.

William Morris

M. B. Grennan, *William Morris: Medievalist and Revolutionary*, 1945.

Graham Hough, *The Last Romantics*, 1949. Contains a good chapter on Morris.

J. W. Mackail, *The Life of William Morris*, 2 vols., 1899. Though a lengthy work, this is the best life and it is also valuable for information on the Pre-Raphaelite Movement.

Algernon Charles Swinburne

Douglas Bush, *Mythology and the Romantic Tradition*, 1937. This is an important book, and the chapter on Swinburne provides a highly unsympathetic account.

T. S. Eliot, *The Sacred Wood*, 1920. One of the most important critics of our century provides an interesting estimate in his essay "Swinburne as a Poet". This essay is also in Eliot's *Selected Essays*, 1932.

G. Lafourcade, *Swinburne: A Literary Biography*, 1932.

Edith Sitwell, *Atlantic Book of British and American Poetry*, 1958. In the Preface to this collection there is a brief and very enthusiastic account of Swinburne.

E. M. W. Tillyard, *Five Poems*, 1948. Contains an essay on "Hertha".

Gerard Manley Hopkins

W. H. Gardner, *G. M. Hopkins: A Study of Poetic Idiosyncrasy in Relation to Poetic Tradition*, 2 vols., 1944. This is a very elaborate and complete study of Hopkins, one that is indispensable.

Alan Heuser, *The Shaping Vision of Gerard Manley Hopkins*, 1958. Heuser, in this recent study, examines Hopkins' poetry in light of his poetic theory.

The Kenyon Review, Summer and Autumn, 1944. Contains a series of critical essays on Hopkins by well-known American critics.

G. F. Lahey, *Gerard Manley Hopkins*, 1930. A biography.

Eleanor Ruggles, *Gerard Manley Hopkins*, 1944. A biography.

Elizabeth Barrett Browning

Osbert Burdett, *The Browning's*, 1929. A biography.

Sir Henry Jones, "Robert Browning and Elizabeth Barrett Browning," in *The Cambridge History of English Literature*, vol. XIII, 1917. Provides a critical estimate.

Gardner B. Taplin, *The Life of Elizabeth Barrett Browning*, 1957.

Virginia Woolf, *Flush: A Biography*, 1933.

Christina Rossetti

C. M. Bowra, *The Romantic Imagination*, 1949. Contains a discussion of her poetry.

Virginia Woolf, *The Second Common Reader*, 1932. A noted author provides a stimulating essay in this book on the poetess.

Marya Zaturenska, *Christina Rossetti: A Portrait with Background*, 1949. This is a very recent and valuable biography.

George Meredith

Lionel Stevenson, *The Ordeal of George Meredith*, 1953.

Edward Fitzgerald

A. J. Arberry, *The Romance of the Rubaiyat*, 1959.

A. McKinley Terhune, *The Life of Edward Fitzgerald*, 1947.

Arthur Hugh Clough

J. I. Osborne, *Arthur Hugh Clough*, 1920.

William Ernest Henley

Jerome H. Buckley, *William Ernest Henley: A Study of the "Counter-Decadence" of the Nineties*, 1945.

Francis Thompson

Paul van K. Thomson, *Francis Thompson: A Critical Biography*, 1961.

T. H. Wright, *Francis Thompson and His Poetry*, 1927.

Edward Lear

Angus Davidson, *Edward Lear: Landscape Painter and Nonsense Poet*, 1938.

Lewis Carroll

Derek Hudson, *Lewis Carroll*, 1954.

Elizabeth Sewell, *The Field of Nonsense*, 1952.

Oscar Wilde

Vyvyan Holland, *Oscar Wilde, a Pictorial Biography*, 1960.

Hesketh Pearson, *The Life of Oscar Wilde, His Life and Wit*, 1946.

Edouard Roditi, *Oscar Wilde*, 1947.

Ernest Dowson

J. M. Longaker, *Ernest Dowson*, 1944.

Lionel Johnson

B. Ifor Evans, *English Poetry in the Later Nineteenth Century*, 1933. Chapter XV provides a critical estimate of Johnson.

The bibliography provided here is necessarily quite selective, and attention should be drawn to the fact that there are many other valuable studies of the period and of individual authors. The student should consult his library catalogue, or the bibliographical information provided in a good history of literature, such as *A Literary History of England*, ed. Albert C. Baugh. *The Victorian Poets, A Guide to research*, ed. F. E. Faverty, 1956 and *Bibliographies of Studies in Victorian Literature* 1945-1954, ed. Austin Wright, are both extremely valuable. Lists of Victorian studies are published each year in *Studies in Philology, Publications of the Modern Language Association*, and in *Victorian Studies*.

www.ingramcontent.com/pod-product-compliance
Lightning Source LLC
LaVergne TN
LVHW021719060526
838200LV00050B/2745